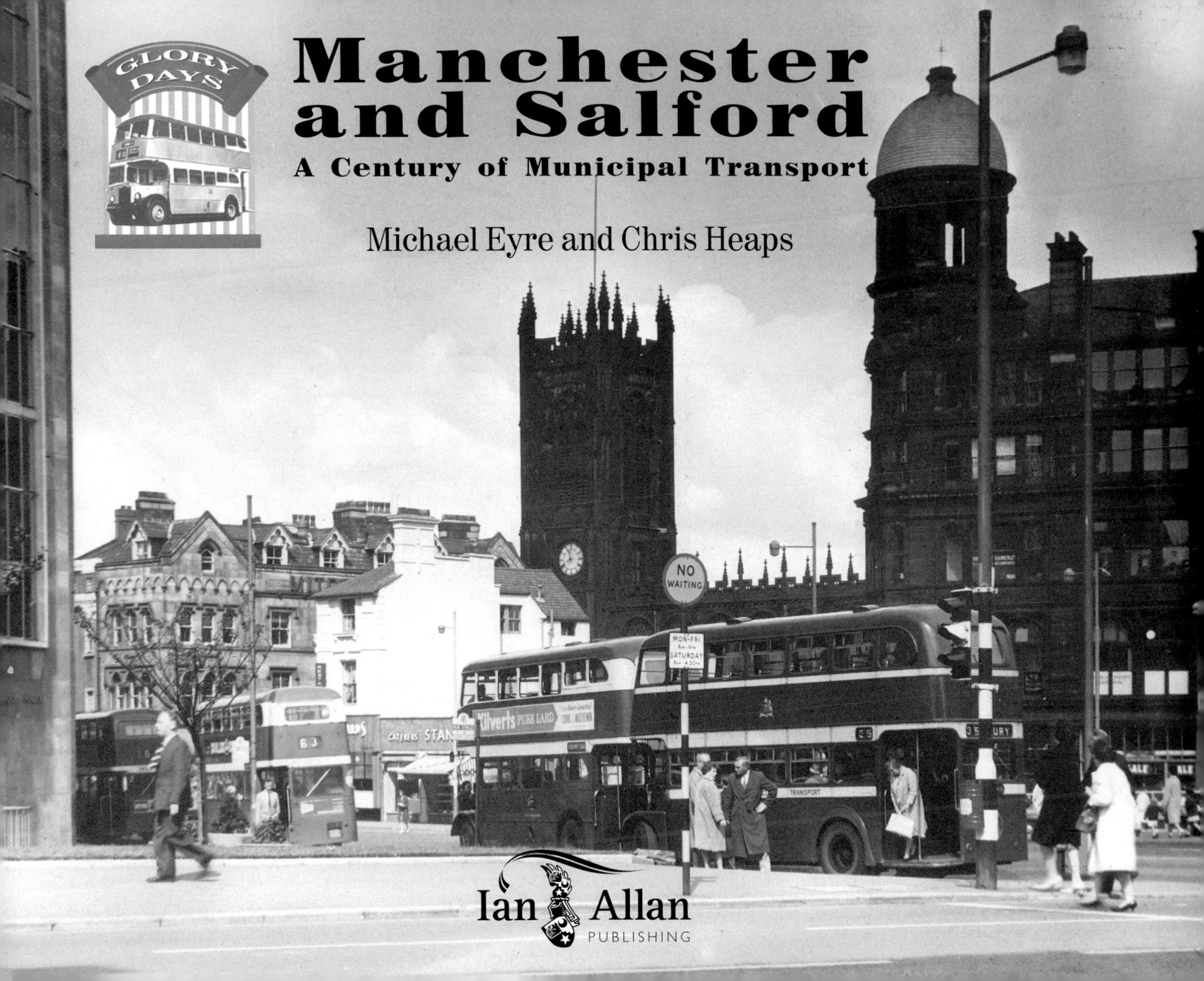
GLORY DAYS
Manchester and Salford
A Century of Municipal Transport
Michael Eyre and Chris Heaps
NO WAITING
MON-FRI
SATURDAY
Kilverts PURE LARD
CATERERS
TRANSPORT
Ian Allan
PUBLISHING

Front cover:
The 'glory buses' of the two cities. Salford Metro-Cammell-bodied Daimler CVG6 511, on service 84 from the city, stops outside the Trafford Park Hotel in Third Avenue, Trafford Park and is overtaken by Manchester Leyland PD2 3245, also bodied by Metro-Cammell, working the famous 53 service. New in 1951 both were in continuous all-day front line city service for almost 20 years. *N. R. Knight*

Back cover:
The next stop along Third Avenue, Trafford Park from the one on the cover was Metropolitan Vickers' works, later GEC and more recently Alsthom. More than 450 buses operated the rush hour services to the park in the 1940s and 1950s and even in the 1960s some 290 were needed. This picture shows three of them attending a GEC open day in July 1986 after they had passed into preservation. Manchester Burlingham-bodied Leyland PD2/40 3496, Salford Metro-Cammell-bodied Daimler CVG6 112 and similarly bodied Manchester PD2/12 3460, new 1957, 1962 and 1956 respectively. *Ted Gray*

Contents

	Introduction and Acknowledgements	3
1.	Horse Power	4
2.	Electric Trams	7
3.	Buses	14
4.	The Glorious Pilcher Years	23
5.	Wartime	32
6.	Glory Days in Salford	36
7.	Bridges — the 57/77 and 95/96	42
8.	Tough Times for Everyone	44
9.	The 1960s — Decade of Change	47
	Colour photographs	49
10.	Glory Days in Manchester	97
11.	Sunglow Sunset	100
	Further reading	100
	The Fleets	101

Title page:
Manchester's Cannon Street bus station in 1961, looking from Corporation Street across to the Cathedral. A Salford Daimler CVG6, bound for Bury on service 35, has drawn up behind a Manchester Leyland PD1 from the 3100-series, waiting to depart on service 4 to Bamford. Metro-Cammell Orion-bodied Leyland PD2 fleetnumber 3555 is going to Heywood on service 63 and ahead of it is another PD2 from the 3411 batch on the 26 to Moston. *MCT*

First published 2001

ISBN 0 7110 2790 0

Published by Ian Allan Publishing

an imprint of Ian Allan Publishing Ltd, Hersham, Surrey KT12 4RG.

Printed by Ian Allan Printing Ltd, Hersham, Surrey KT12 4RG.

Code: 0105/B2

Introduction

Commissioned by Ian Allan Publishing to commemorate the Manchester Museum of Transport's celebration of the 100th anniversary of the commencement of municipal passenger transport services in Manchester and Salford, this is a story about the good days of the passenger transport undertakings of the cities of Manchester and Salford — inevitably touching on a few of the less happy times as well. It is not a history of either, for that has been covered more than adequately in a range of books on their tramways and buses.

Much of the story revolves around the general managers, for it is personalities and people that build organisations and give them their special character. There are examples of leadership, of innovations and interesting parallels in the achievement of co-ordination followed by separation, often as a result of traffic congestion, but sometimes as a result of civic pride and ambition. To quote the old proverb, we shall see history repeating itself.

It is important to bear in mind that Manchester Corporation Transport Department's fleet (about 1,500 buses in the 1950s) was some five times the size of that of Salford (about 320) and its actions, industry influences and general visibility were proportionally the greater. Besides those of the two cities, many other operators' buses worked into Manchester and Salford on joint services but this is a book about the fleets of Manchester and Salford, and those who seek pictures of other joint operators' vehicles in the cities or those of the Passenger Transport Executive will have to wait until another book comes along.

Acknowledgements

The photographers, in particular Peter Roberts, John Ryan, Neville Knight, Roy Marshall, Arnold Richardson and the late Reg Wilson, have enabled us to cover almost all of the postwar vehicle types plus a few prewar ones in colour. One or two pictures are imperfect because the film is old; we used them because they give a unique record.

We had generous contributions from Geoff Burrows, Ted Gray, Stephen Morris, Ralph Oakes-Garnett, David Potts, Dennis Talbot, George Turnbull, Keith Walker, Paul Williams and David Young. The records and publications of the Omnibus Society and the PSV Circle were invaluable. Colleagues at the Museum of Transport provided much help; many of the pictures attributed to Manchester or Salford Corporation are in the museum's archives.

Years ago when he worked for the Department, John Miller arranged the preservation of the Manchester fleet records. Equally long since, general managers Charles Baroth, Jack Thompson and John Craggs, and the directors of the SELNEC and Greater Manchester PTEs gave us access to records and direct personal help.

Three old friends gave special support — Alan Townsin's wise guidance was invaluable, Peter Greaves spent weeks meticulously checking everything line by line and Eric Baroth, son of Salford's highly respected general manager, provided unique insights.

We thank them all.

Michael Eyre, Chris Heaps
December 2000

1. Horse Power

KEYDATES

1824 1 Jan – Greenwood starts horse omnibus Pendleton-Manchester

1865 – Manchester Carriage Co formed led by Greenwood, red and white livery

1870 – Tramways Act: municipalities can construct but must lease the operation

1872: 18 Aug – Public horsetram operation starts in the two cities

1888 – Fixed stopping places and Kay's fare box introduced

1890 – Fleet of 385 horsetrams

1893 – Bill to allow local authorities to operate trams

1896 – Manchester Corporation Bill to operate trams within or beyond the city boundary – Salford, Stockport, Ashton, Oldham decide to operate their own

1898 – Sample MCT cars ordered from Carriage & Tramways Co, Hurst Nelson, Brush, Ashbury's, Milnes

There is an old saying that 'What Manchester does today, the world does tomorrow'. If one includes Salford and changes the timescale to 'five years later', then it certainly applies to road passenger transport.

On 1 January 1824 John Greenwood, proprietor of the tollgates at Stretford and Pendleton, began a horsebus service from Pendleton, Salford to Market Street, Manchester. Quite different from the existing stage and mail coach services, which were longer in distance, expensive and on which pre-booking was the rule, Greenwood's service covered only some two and a half miles, had a fare of 6d (2.5p), operated several times a day and picked up any passengers anywhere en route. It was a great success. Five years later George Shillibeer did the same in London.

Greenwood introduced more services serving most of the then suburbs — Rusholme, Ardwick, Broughton, Cheetham Hill, Eccles, Greenheys — and by 1850 had some 64 horsebuses, mainly 12-seaters, with a coachbuilding and repair works at Ford Lane, Pendleton. Inevitably this attracted competition. The principal source commenced in 1852 and was run by a Scotsman. Although there were some modern-day parallels in the introduction of bigger buses and lower fares, the entrepreneur's name was neither Lockhead nor Souter; it was McEwen. Financed by Manchester businessmen, McEwen's firm grew into the City Omnibus Co Ltd. Greenwood's response (by this time the business was run by his son) was to follow suit and in 1865 the principal firms merged to form The Manchester Carriage Company, with a fleet of 91 vehicles and John Greenwood junior as managing director. The cities of Manchester and Salford now had a single, co-ordinated transport system that ignored the artificial demarcation of civic boundaries. In 1870 184 vehicles were needed for daytime service.

The 1870 Tramways Act was to preserve and improve this situation, for whilst it empowered local authorities to construct tramways, it did not allow them to operate the tramcars. Both cities decided to construct tramways and in 1876 bids were sought for their operation. There was a slight perturbation when the successful tenderers were not the Manchester Carriage Company but the firm of Busby & Turton, which already operated in other cities. In the event

A Manchester Carriage & Tramways Company two-horse car at the Harpurhey terminus on Rochdale Road, outside the Farmer's Arms. 'For Boggart Hole Clough' reads the board on the side but visitors would have a half-mile walk to the municipal park of that name and a steep climb back to catch the tram home. *Museum of Transport archive*

Tram P.14 from the Pendleton division of the Carriage Company is an Eades reversible car, the body being turned on a pivot in the truck at termini. The Manchester and Salford licence numbers can be seen just in front of the staircase. The tram is turning from Station Road into Chorley Road, Swinton, having travelled out of the city via Pendlebury — the same loop was used by the much later joint 57/77 bus service. *Museum of Transport archive*

The smaller type of Carriage Company horsebus at Cheadle, Cheshire on the service to the tram terminus at Palatine Road, West Didsbury. *C. W. Heaps collection*

they arranged for continued operation by the Carriage Company. There was considerable legal wrangling between the corporations and the other parties, including the formation of the Manchester Suburban Tramways Company to protect the Carriage Company's interests outside the city, and it was not until 1890 that the contract was transferred. Meantime, the tramways opened in 1877 and in 1880 the company was reconstituted as the Manchester Carriage & Tramways Co Ltd (colloquially 'the Carriage Company').

The company's comprehensive horsebus and tram network covered the whole of the conurbation of those days, with services to Broughton, Cheetham Hill, Hightown, Pendleton, Swinton, Peel Green, Greenheys, Moss Side, Stretford, Fallowfield, West Didsbury, Stockport, Denton, Ashton-under-Lyne, Hollinwood, Oldham, Waterhead and Harpurhey, with a typical frequency of every five minutes. There were also one or two inter-suburb horsebus services — Moss Side to Chorlton for example. Glory days indeed.

There was a flaw in this network that would plague the Manchester system for the next 80 years. There were no cross-city services, routes terminated at Piccadilly, Exchange, Albert Square and Deansgate. The cause was traffic congestion in Manchester's Piccadilly and Market Street. One tram a minute passed down Market Street in 1890 but by 1899 this had grown to one every 12 seconds and the police and others were objecting to the congestion caused by the trams.

Salford had no natural city centre of its own and therefore all the services from Salford crossed the civic boundary (in the city centre this is the River Irwell) to terminate in Manchester. Because of the congestion in Market Street, they stopped in Deansgate or St Mary's Gate — the latter was often referred to as 'Exchange', the name covering the nearby Royal Exchange and the not quite so nearby Exchange Station. An ambitious Manchester Corporation would exploit this short distance crossing of its city boundary in the coming years.

The Municipal Corporations Association Act of 1893 empowered municipalities to operate their tramways. Both cities determined so to do and in 1895 held talks as to how this should be organised. Salford wanted a joint board but Manchester had other ideas. Manchester's goal was nothing less than to run the whole network itself, including the lines in Oldham, Ashton, Swinton, Stockport, Stretford, Eccles, Swinton & Pendlebury, Prestwich — and Salford. A shocked Salford discovered that for some months previously Manchester had been secretly discussing this plan with the surrounding authorities. Discussion between the two cities ceased; there would be no joint board and from this point onwards (and indeed until SELNEC had been established for some years) there was to be an atmosphere of mutual suspicion and jealousy between the two in any matters concerning transport.

In fact, the joint board idea would not have worked — for whilst Salford's vision was 50/50 membership, Manchester's

A lesser-known invention of Manchester Corporation was vehicle preservation. In 1916 it retained the last of the horsebuses bought from the Carriage Company. Carefully stored, fleetnumber 2 was used on suitable civic occasions and passed to SELNEC and Greater Manchester Transport. It was then placed in the Museum of Transport, where it underwent a thorough professional restoration. This picture shows it in St Peter's Square on 10 October 1974 en route to an open day at Hyde Road Works. *N. R. Knight*

ideas were based on size and mileage. This implied something more like 80/20, which meant that it would have dominated with Salford having little say in anything.

Ashton, Oldham, Salford and Stockport soon decided to operate their own tramways. There was an oddity in Stockport, where Manchester built and paid for the whole of the line to that town, and it remained Manchester's until 1923 when the lease expired and it became jointly operated. Eccles and Swinton & Pendlebury threw in their lot with Salford — geography ensured that they had little choice — and Manchester took the rest: Audenshaw, Denton, Droylsden, Failsworth, Gorton, Heaton Norris, Levenshulme, Moss Side and Stretford. It would add Altrincham, Sale and Middleton later. It also signed up Prestwich but was to be frustrated in this by a disagreement with Salford.

So was cast a pattern which would last until SELNEC — an expansive Manchester always looking beyond its city boundaries to provide an integrated network and Salford operating within its more limited area, hemmed in by geography and other operators, principally Lancashire United. Separating the two in the city centre was the River Irwell — which many Salford routes would continue to cross in order to terminate in or pass along Deansgate. Manchester worried about the lack of cross-city services but their expansion was inhibited by the Market Street traffic problems and in so far as any west of Deansgate were concerned, there was little enthusiasm from Salford.

The Carriage Company viewed all this with alarm — when the corporations took over, its business would vanish, as would the integrated network. It tried hard to argue its case, going to the extent of promoting its own parliamentary bill to continue operations but the two corporations ensured the bill's defeat and in 1897 were granted the necessary powers to build and operate their own tramways. Both would build fine electric tramway networks but the glory days of an integrated system were lost.

An 1880 traffic jam in Piccadilly and Market Street, with three Carriage Company horsebuses, 24 horsetrams and numerous other slow-moving vehicles. Little wonder that the police began to object. This picture shows why so many Manchester and Salford services were kept away from Market Street and why there were so few cross-city routes. *Museum of Transport archive*

2. Electric Trams

The necessary parliamentary permissions having been obtained, the two cities proceeded with the necessary track work, overhead wiring, electrical installations and the purchase of trams. Manchester bought six experimental cars to assess various manufacturers' products but, whilst it was evaluating them, other municipalities got ahead in the delivery queue and the choice of builder for both cities was limited to those that could supply in time. Manchester's initial orders for 430 cars, including 25 single-deckers for what would become the famous 53 service, went to Brush and Milnes, whilst Salford's first 130 also came from Milnes.

The Manchester single-deckers were of a somewhat unusual design. Known as combination or 'California' cars, they had open driving platforms, partitioned from open loading platforms with seats (for smokers) and a closed centre section. The name came from the California Street cable cars in San Francisco, which were of this layout — and still were in 2000AD.

Until electrification was complete and enough electric cars were available, the horsetrams continued to operate. Salford chose to buy sufficient of these, plus horses, to work its lines. Conversely, Manchester arranged for the Carriage Company to

KEYDATES

1901 – General Managers appointed – SCT E. Hatton, MCT J. M. McElroy
Feb – first MCT car delivered to part-completed Queens Road depot
28 Apr – Manchester and Salford take over the tramways
7 Jun – first MCT electric tram in public service
28 Jun – Deansgate dispute, Salford to be stopped from crossing River Irwell
4 Oct – Salford electric tramways open

continued

▲ ◄ Two California cars — a Manchester one from the 512-536 class new in 1903 and long since scrapped, and a San Francisco California Street cable-car still at work in 1985. The Board of Trade objected to the risks of having passengers seated alongside the driver and the bulkheads of the Manchester cars were moved to provide backwards- and forwards-facing seats on the entrance platform. Manchester 765 is preserved and operates on the short tramway in the city's Heaton Park. *MCT, D. M. Eyre*

KEYDATES continued

1902 Dec – Hyde Road depot pressed into use, part completed

1903 31 Mar – last horsetram in Manchester
31 May – Deansgate dispute resolved, SCT starts to use Deansgate

1905 Apr – MCT parcels service starts
– Salford Manager E. Hatton resigns, G. W. Holford appointed

1906 Jul – MCT first three motorbuses delivered and start operation

1907 Apr – MCT decides to build complete trams in Car Works – order for 50

1909 Jul – Princess Road depot opened (250-295 cars). First complete tram built in Car Works

1912 – SCT livery changed from maroon and white to red and white

continue to operate the horsetram services until the lines were electrified. It bought the horsebuses together with 11 trams and the necessary horses. These trams worked the lines from St Mary's Gate to Regent Bridge and the city boundary on Bury New Road during the about to be related dispute with Salford and thereafter were used temporarily on other lines during electrification work. Manchester's first electric trams ran in June 1901 and Salford's followed in October.

Manchester and the Carriage Company then got into a dispute over how compensation Manchester should pay to the company and for what items, the argument stemming from the Corporation's frustration in not gaining total control. It was eventually settled and the Carriage Company was wound up in 1903, returning the for then handsome sum of £1,167,965 to its shareholders, who then formed the Manchester Carriage Co (1903) Ltd to operate taxis, private hire and funeral services. The firm continued into the 1960s; much later its founding father was commemorated on Metrolink tram 1024 which bears his name.

More serious were the disputes between the two cities. The first started in 1901 before any of the electric tram services had commenced and concerned the Bury New Road/Prestwich service. The first mile or so out of the city was in Manchester along Great Ducie Street and Bury New Road, passing Strangeways Gaol and the equally famous Boddington's Brewery. There was then just over a mile of Salford to the Prestwich boundary and, having made an agreement in principle with Prestwich, Manchester proposed to work the service. Salford disagreed and outwitted Manchester by quickly constructing a line entirely in Salford, via Blackfriars Road, Clowes Street and Great Cheetham Street West to join Bury New Road a couple of streets beyond the Manchester boundary. It was the first line to open in Salford. In due course, Salford would also work the original route and 54 years later both routes would become part of the joint 95/96 bus service. This loss of Prestwich was a major setback for Manchester and, not surprisingly, it provoked a ferocious reaction from the larger city.

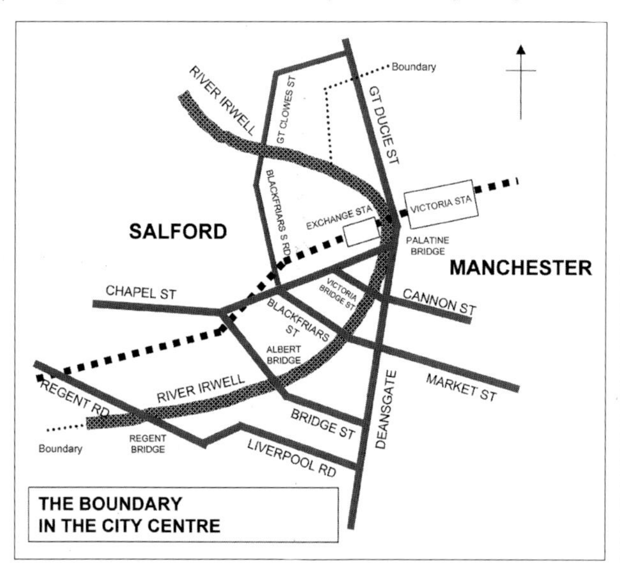

THE BOUNDARY IN THE CITY CENTRE

Salford's plan was that all its services would run from one side of Salford to the other, passing in both directions along Manchester's Deansgate tracks, crossing the Irwell at Regent Bridge, Albert Bridge, Blackfriars Bridge, Victoria Bridge, Palatine Bridge or the boundary north of Strangeways on Bury New Road. Both parties were agreed that Salford should pay for use of Manchester's tracks. Stung by the Bury New Road dispute, Manchester stipulated that in addition it would decide which route each individual Salford service should use to enter and leave Deansgate and how often each should run. For example, Salford planned that the Eccles New Road services would travel via Oldfield Road, Chapel Street and Bridge Street, whilst Manchester required that they should use Regent Road, Regent Bridge and Liverpool Road.

Salford, of course, declined and Manchester's draconian response was to refuse to allow any Salford trams to cross the boundary and enter the city. Thus, at very short notice, Salford had to re-cast all its proposed services to run to and terminate at the boundary on Blackfriars Bridge — not a wide thoroughfare, arriving Salford cars had to unload quickly, reverse and leave promptly to avoid complete blockage. Arriving passengers then had to walk the few hundred yards into the city centre, whilst departing passengers huddled without shelter on the bridge. This ludicrous situation lasted from October 1901 until the end of May 1903, when Salford agreed to pay a higher rate per car mile to Manchester in exchange for the choice of route. The affair created additional, long-lasting ill feeling between the city councils, their transport committees and transport departments, and also from the citizens of Salford at large.

There was one final episode in the boundary saga. It took place 22 years later and concerned the clearance beneath the

Victoria Station railway arch over Great Ducie Street, which was used by Manchester and Salford cars. This was too low for closed-top tramcars and both corporations used open-top trams on services that passed beneath it. In 1925, tired of passenger complaints, Salford bought six special low-height closed-top cars (225-230). No sooner had they entered service than the Manchester Corporation Highways Department and the Manchester Corporation Tramways Department arrived with picks, shovels, new rails, a tar boiler and a steamroller, and proceeded to lower the roadway, allowing any tram to pass and rendering Salford's purchase unnecessary.

◂ The dispute during which Salford cars were banned from Manchester tracks having been resolved after some two years, this 1904 picture shows the seeds of the longer-lasting issue of traffic congestion which would, in time, cause the splitting of the joint 57/77 bus services. Four Salford and one Manchester trams make their way south along Deansgate, others going north can be seen in the distance and there would be many more tramcars behind the photographer. The traffic congestion got progressively worse as buses and motor vehicles became more and more numerous. *Chris Heaps collection*

Arguments apart, both corporations' tramway electrification projects proceeded smoothly and efficiently, opening on 7 June 1901 in Manchester and on 4 October 1901 in Salford. Salford's depot was at Frederick Road and Manchester's first was at Queens Road, the road at the side being named Boyle Street after the enterprising chairman of the Tramways Committee, Daniel Boyle, of whom more anon. Such was the success that Manchester's second depot and works at Hyde Road had to be pressed into use uncompleted in 1902. The two corporations took over the private tramways of Trafford Park Estates Ltd in 1904, the cars passing to Salford.

A Carriage Company enterprise continued by Manchester was the parcels service —there was a legal challenge by commercial operators as to the Corporation's right to do this but it won the day. Using trams, motor vans and handcarts, it served Manchester and its suburbs and, somewhat surprisingly, Salford. Highly successful, the van service continued into SELNEC days, the fleet of about 50 continuing to live up to the service's 1905 slogan 'Quick Collection, Rapid Transit and Prompt Delivery'.

In 1907 with the new Car Works adjoining Hyde Road depot in full operation, the Manchester transport committee decided to build complete tramcars. The first order was for 50 and thereafter until the Second World War a proportion of new tram and bus bodies was built in the Car Works. The first Car Works tram was completed in 1909 and Princess Road depot opened in the same year.

By 1912 traffic congestion in both Market Street and Deansgate was causing further problems. Already Manchester had started to move some of its tram termini away from the Market Street/Piccadilly area — Stevenson Square terminus opening in 1910, for example, but Market Street still had a tram, often a big bogie car, about every 40 seconds in each direction and the Chief Constable was asking for a reduction. Likewise Deansgate but with Salford's services already in place there was no simple way of easing the congestion.

◂ The parcels delivery service was a feature of Manchester's operations which continued into SELNEC days. As Salford did not provide a similar facility, there was no dispute about the area it covered or the text on the vans, which in prewar days carried strong marketing messages. This is a Ford Model B new in October 1935. *MCT*

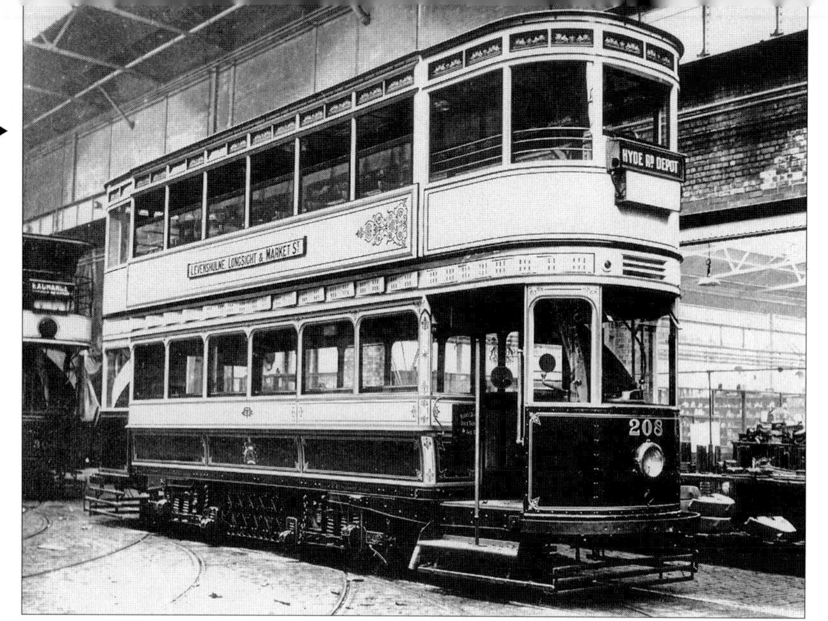

Manchester bogie car 208, built by Brush in 1903, in the Car Works, having just been repainted. The picture was probably taken after completion of its rebuilding with a closed roof and platforms. The Manchester tramcar livery was unusual in having the darker colour on the lowest side panels — in most fleets, including Salford, the lowest panel was the lighter colour. *MCT*

The Docks terminus in Ordsall Lane with Salford single-truck car 155 and a bogie car behind it, both cars were built by Brush. The picture was taken after the joint Manchester and Salford agreement for a single series of tram service numbers, and number indicators have been added to the Salford cars. The 70 and 71 circulars kept their numbers when converted to buses on 31 March 1947 — they were Salford Corporation's last tram routes. *Museum of Transport archive*

Salford's original livery was maroon and off-white, contrasting with Manchester's vermilion and white which had been inherited from the Carriage Company — both liveries being ornately lined out in gold, blue and other colours. In 1912 the Salford transport committee took the curious decision to change to red and white, making its cars the same as Manchester's to a casual observer. What Manchester thought of this is not recorded.

Both corporations introduced numbers for the tram services in 1914. Manchester's was a simple series starting at 10. Salford, however, chose to use what it called a 'destination number'. Prefixed with an 'S' for Salford, the number did indeed refer to the destination and each route had at least two numbers, one for each end, trams showing a different number in each direction. The scheme proved so hard to understand that it was given up after eight months and the trams reverted to showing destination and 'via'. Manchester introduced suffix letters for short workings in 1919 and there things rested until 1926 when, pressured by bus competition, some cross-city tram services were started. These brought Manchester cars, with service numbers, into Salford and the two operators agreed upon a co-ordinated numbering system for the tram services. Manchester's kept their existing numbers, which went from 10 to 59, and Salford's were numbered from 61 to 83. Bus service numbers were introduced in 1930 but there was no co-ordination between the two operators, other than

for jointly operated services. Manchester's bus service numbers duplicated those of its tram services and at one stage the corporation had quite different trolleybus, tram and motorbus services all with the same service number.

The joint cross-city trams were 33 (Swinton-Reddish), 34 (Weaste-Belle Vue), 36 (Kersal-Levenshulme), 37 (Prestwich-Levenshulme) plus a cross-suburb route from Pendleton to Stretford (58). All except the 58 were short-lived, being split in 1930 because of traffic congestion in Market Street, apart from odd journeys on 34, 36 and 37, which ran until 1936/7. The 33 and 37 and their demise were, in some way, an interesting forerunner of the later 57/77 and 95/96 bus services. The 58 was an early conversion to buses and survived into SELNEC days.

Salford suffered a serious blow in 1928 when fire destroyed its transport offices in Blackfriars — everything was lost right down to tickets. Bury, Bolton and Lancashire United (but not Manchester) sent some of their own ticket stocks which Salford used until replacements could be delivered. The offices were not rebuilt but were moved to Frederick Road since extra depot accommodation was being built at Weaste, which opened in 1929.

The general managers of the two undertakings changed in the mid-1920s. Salford had already had one change in 1905, when G. W. Holford replaced Ernest Hatton, and he in turn was succeeded by James Moffet in 1924. During this period J. M. McElroy was in charge at Manchester but stress and ill health caused him to retire in 1922 and his Chief Engineer, Henry Mattinson, took over. Being one of the country's largest passenger transport undertakings, the Manchester post was a 'top job' and Henry Mattinson was the first of four Manchester

◄ Outbound for Chorlton via All Saints, Manchester bogie car 803 outside the Palace Theatre, Oxford Street at the junction with Whitworth Street West in the late 1920s. The cenotaph in St Peter's Square can be seen in the far background; the Central Reference Library had not been built at that time. *MCT*

▲
Salford and Manchester tramcars at the Market Street end of Piccadilly, with the Ryland's building in the background. Salford car 215 is en route to Weaste from Belle Vue on the cross-city service, the Manchester cars (885 and 814) are on the 31 (Fairfield-Chorlton) service. The picture is said to have been taken on 25 July 1937, the last day of through operation of the trams. *Museum of Transport archive*

general managers who were to make major impacts on the whole bus industry. The others were Stuart Pilcher, Albert Neal and Ralph Bennett. We use the word 'bus' purposely, for although Henry Mattinson was above all a tramway man, he saw the opportunity afforded by the motorbus and grasped it. Salford's post-war manager, Charles Baroth, would become noted not only for his rescue of the Salford bus fleet, as we shall see, but also for what was perhaps the most immaculate fleet of municipal buses in the country.

Over the next 40-odd years, Manchester's general managers — Mattinson, Pilcher, Neal and Bennett — would lead the industry's way with, successively, express inter-town bus services, which kept the independent and company operators at bay, the adoption of diesel engines, metal-framed bus bodies, eight-foot-wide buses and one-man double-deckers. After retirement Stuart Pilcher was asked by the government to become Chairman of the West Midlands Traffic Commissioners. A later government would recruit Albert Neal to advise upon and help define the PTEs, and Ralph Bennett would become Chief Executive at London Transport, sadly in his case only to be beset by political problems. Their relationship with the Manchester Tramways (later Transport) Committee was almost always excellent — not so the City Council. Henry Mattinson's first argument with that body was in the mid-1920s and only Ralph Bennett had a really smooth tenure.

The tramways settled down to busy and generally profitable operations. There was the usual rebuilding of tramcars — adding top covers, balcony covers, enclosed platforms, and buying or building extra or replacement cars. However, Henry Mattinson died suddenly in 1928 from complications arising from malaria and his successor, Stuart Pilcher, encouraged by certain councillors and aldermen, was to change all that.

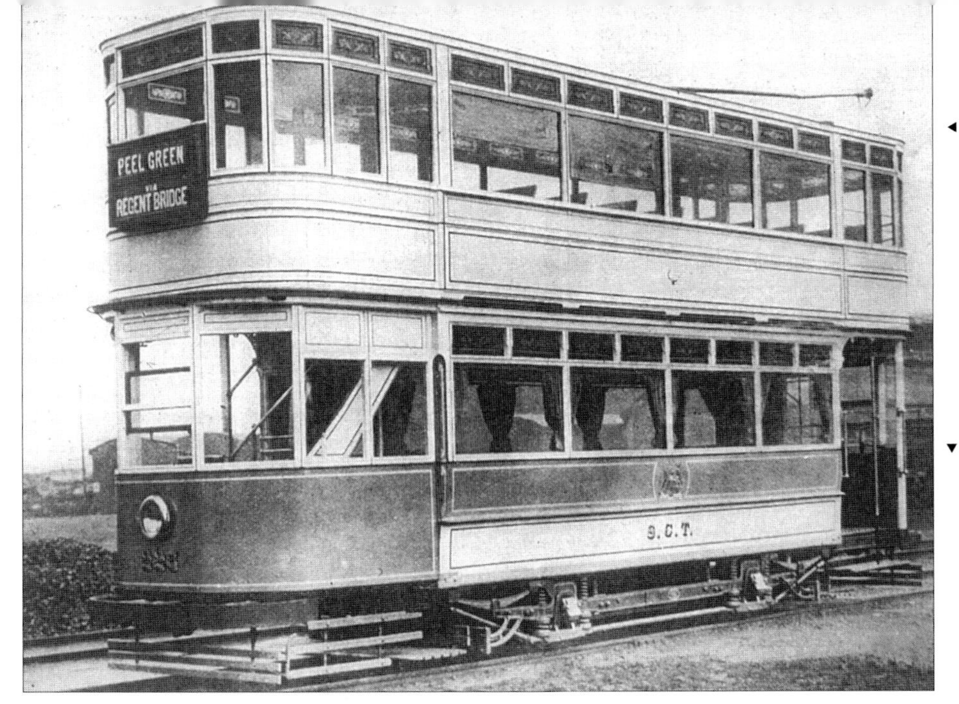

◄ In 1925 Salford bought six cars of specially reduced overall height to enable them to pass beneath the Victoria Station railway arches over Great Ducie Street, until then restricted to open-top cars. This track was part of the Manchester system and no sooner had Salford taken delivery, than the City of Manchester Highways Department turned out with picks, shovels and a steam roller to lower the roadway and thereby provide clearance for any closed-top car — Manchester or Salford. This picture shows 225 when new, complete with lower-deck curtains and the abbreviated fleetname on its rocker panels. *SCT*

▼ Often forgotten is that one of Stuart Pilcher's first actions at Manchester was the building of 38 new tramcars. Officially titled 'Pullman', to his intense annoyance they were usually known as 'Pilchers'. The design was a mixture of a modern upper-deck and old-fashioned lower-deck that used parts from the trams they replaced. Their single trucks did not run well on Manchester tracks, resulting in a yawing and pitching motion that earned them the nickname of 'Rockers'. All were sold for further service in 1946-1948 to Leeds (7), Aberdeen (6), Sunderland (14) and Edinburgh (11). This picture shows fleetnumber 176 in Hyde Road depot, about to work the cross-city Manchester/Salford service from Belle Vue to Weaste. *MCT*

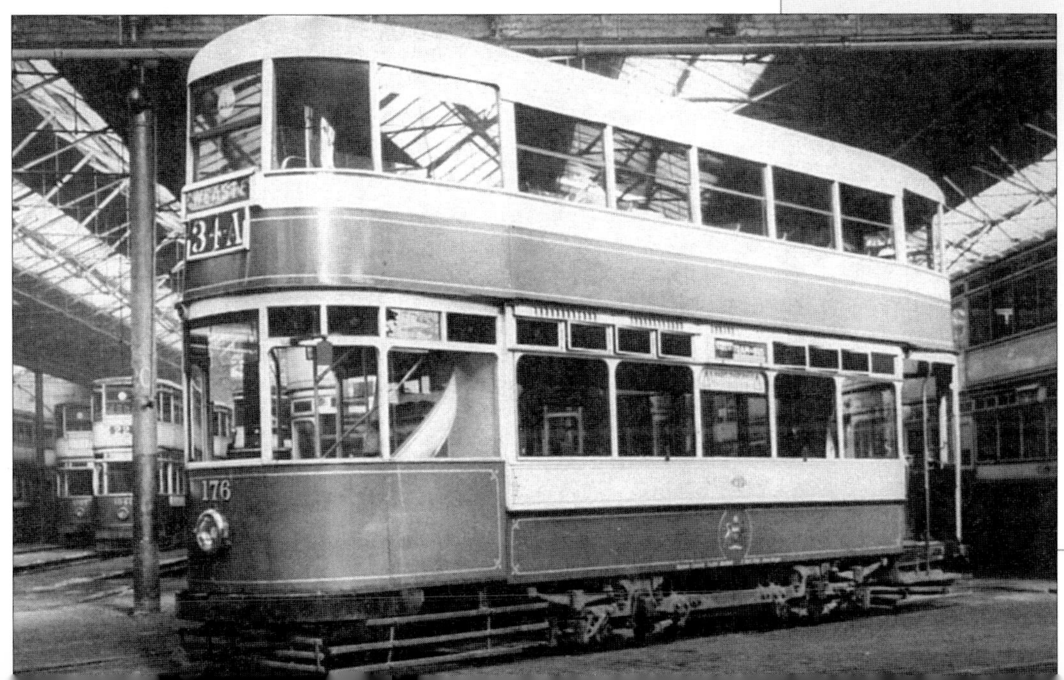

KEYDATES

1920 Jul – first SCT motorbus

1922 – J. M. McElroy retires due to ill health, H. Mattinson appointed MCT general manager

1924 – SCT manager G. W. Holford resigns, J. S. D. Moffet appointed

1925 – SCT tram fleet reaches peak of 230 cars
– MCT Princess Road central reservation tram track opened

1926 – MCT Kingsway central reservation tram track opened
– MCT open Parrs Wood bus garage
Aug – joint numbering for tram services, MCT below 61, SCT 61-83 up, not for buses
Aug – Cross-city Manchester-Salford trams

1927 Apr – First express bus service
Dec – 12 express services involving Manchester, Ashton, Bolton, Bury, LUT, Oldham, Rochdale, Salford, Stockport

continued

3. Buses

Manchester was not early into the motorbus field. It had a Critchley-Norris on loan for a short period in 1904 and bought three Crossley-engined Leylands in 1906. Nothing strange about that choice — the long-established Manchester firm of Crossley Brothers Ltd, parent company of Crossley Motors Ltd, was an engine manufacturer with an enviable reputation for excellence. It supplied Leyland in the latter's early days and, indeed, helped Leyland develop its own engine. What was a surprise in March 1906 was the resignation of Tramways Committee Chairman Dan Boyle to become Managing Director of the newly formed and well-backed Manchester District Motor Omnibus Co Ltd. Its territorial intentions were ambitious and, in retrospect, remarkably similar to the area eventually covered by North Western — Northwich, Knutsford, Alderley, Macclesfield, Buxton, Stockport and the southern suburbs of Manchester. Its garage was in Trafford Park.

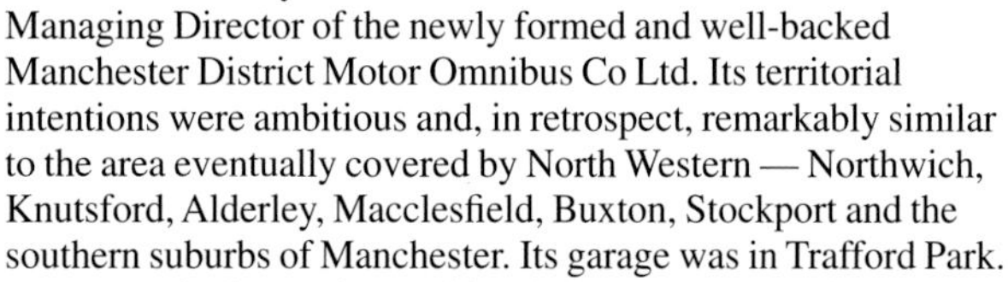

Manchester's reaction to this private upstart was friendly — it assured Manchester District that whilst it did not wish to have a monopoly of bus services, it did propose to operate its own. Given the tramway events of a few years previously, and what happened in the next few months, one might speculate how much economy of truth there was in this seemingly warm welcome.

The company began operations with a fleet of Wolseley buses but made the mistake of selecting affluent areas in which to do so — Chorlton, Didsbury, Alderley Edge. It was promptly attacked for noise, dirt and variations from authorised routes by an influential group of citizens led by Judge Parry. The City's Watch Committee, which issued licences for buses, was persuaded to refuse any renewals and diplomatically asked the Tramways Committee to replace its motorbuses with horsebuses. Defeated,

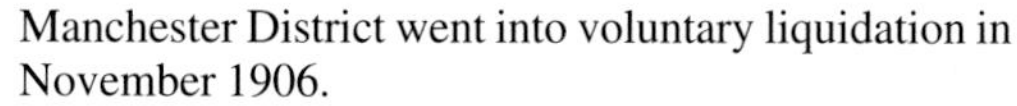

Manchester District went into voluntary liquidation in November 1906.

In 1908 the less well backed but more determined William Stanway appeared. He contrived to beat off Judge Parry and his cohorts, obtained licences and, in consequence, the Corporation's motorbus operations also restarted. Stanway himself ran into financial problems and soon gave up. For the next 20 years the Manchester Corporation bus fleet grew modestly with 'feeder' routes for the tramways (Cheadle-West Didsbury, Northenden-West Didsbury) and inter-suburban routes (Cheetham Hill-Crumpsall, Moston-Brookdale Park, for example).

By virtue of its geography, Salford was well served by its trams and was therefore in no hurry to introduce motorbuses. Its first arrived in 1920, for an inter-suburban route from Pendleton to Great Cheetham Street, and until 1926 the pattern followed that of Manchester. By 1926 Salford had 19 buses and Manchester had 48. The makes were unremarkable for the day — AEC, Bristol, Daimler, Vulcan and Karrier at Manchester; Leyland, Vulcan and Karrier at Salford. Both operators were to be disappointed with the Karrier and in Manchester's case, what

Photographed in the Car Works yard to show the splash guard fitted to its rear wheels, this is Manchester's seventh bus, N 9246, a Daimler CC with bodywork by Dodson. New in September 1913 its chassis was requisitioned by the government for war use in August 1914. The body was put into store and fitted to one of six new Daimler Y-type chassis, released by the government in 1916. *MCT*

Salford 7 (BA 2599), a Leyland O-type with Leyland body new in 1921. *Leyland Motors Ltd*

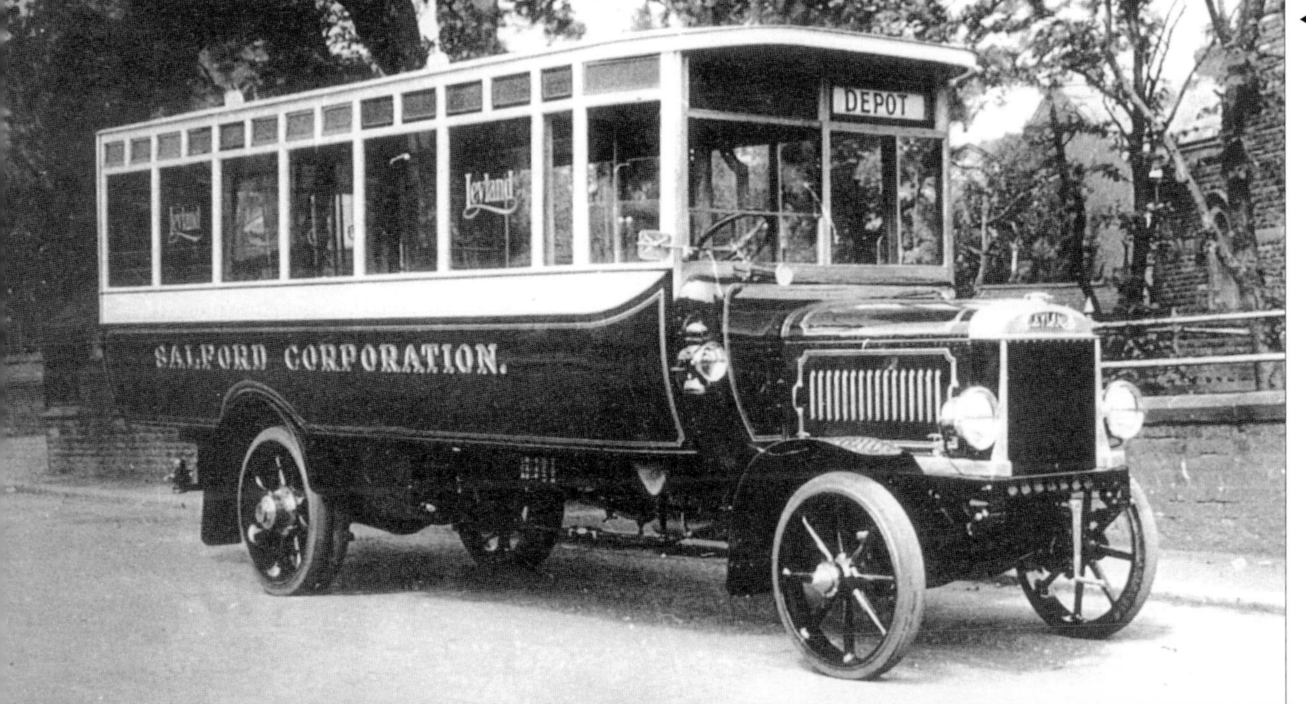

Salford 10 (BA 4147), a Leyland-bodied Leyland G-type, one of a pair bought in 1923. *Leyland Motors Ltd*

No apologies for the poor picture quality of this shot. Taken at West Didsbury in 1925 it shows three of Manchester's buses and a tram. The front bus is 1924 Bristol-bodied Bristol 4-ton ND 8183 bound for Droylsden; behind it, going to Cheadle, is one of the 1925 batch of AEC 401s with Davidson bodies (28-37). The third bus is one of six Karrier JH bought in 1924 and although it has Brooklands on its indicator, it is going nowhere — its bonnet is open and it has broken down. Most of Manchester's unreliable Karriers were part-exchanged in 1928/9 for 14 second-hand Bristol 4-tonners, surplus to the needs of the Sunderland District company. *Harvey Frost*

Manchester's first dedicated bus garage, Parrs Wood, opened in 1926 and the first buses to be delivered new there were 48-56, Daimler CL with Strachan & Brown bodies. They also introduced the 'Edinburgh' rear-entrance. Developed originally by Scottish Motor Traction, it was adopted by Manchester for safety reasons and was a feature of the majority of the corporation's pre-war single-deckers. Another Manchester feature of the time, taken from the tramcars, was the ruby-coloured etched glass of the opening ventilator windows. *MCT*

might be termed emergency action was needed in 1928 when 14 second-hand Bristols were bought to allow disposal of the Karriers.

There was relatively unregulated bus competition in the late 1920s and aggressive private bus operators began to threaten the tramways. The 1926 General Strike produced many new private companies, J. R. Tognarelli of Farnworth for example, and competition became very keen, with the larger ones, such as Ribble and North Western, gaining a hold in many towns. Henry Mattinson took the initiative — if the public wanted fast bus services that competed with the tramcars then the municipalities themselves would provide them and they would do it better than any private firm. Acting with quite remarkable speed, the city and surrounding municipalities set up a network of jointly operated express bus services.

The corporations were not above using some of the independents' tactics to protect their new network — such as starting from private ground, running without local authority licences, 'nursing' a rival's bus and exceeding the speed limit (the corporations paid drivers' fines). A clever feature was 'clockface' timetabling — the services were easy to understand, running every hour, half-hour or quarter-hour. Besides protecting the trams, the express buses proved even more successful in their own right — so much so that Lancashire United joined the scheme as a full partner in 1927, North Western followed in 1928 and, although only peripherally involved, Ribble co-operated.

The agreement provided for two types of service — jointly operated and 'by arrangement', whereby a service was not jointly operated but revenue was shared — North Western's Manchester-Buxton and Manchester-Hayfield services, for example. The joint operation keystone was the principle that when a bus operated in another's area, it did so 'as if it belonged to that operator, who received all the revenues after deduction of the agreed rate for working expenses per vehicle mile'. Made three years before the 1930 Road Traffic Act, the 'Co-ordinated Motor Bus Services' operating agreement was held up by the government as 'a model for others to follow'. Thus the bus and tram networks of the cities and surrounding towns were protected and joint working became the norm. By 1930 there were some 40 services involving 11 operators working in the territories of 47 local authorities in the counties of Lancashire, Yorkshire, Derbyshire and Cheshire. Glory days again.

High frequency express operation placed heavy demands on vehicles and brought about major changes in the bus fleets of the two cities. Both needed new single-deckers quickly — over 80 in Manchester's case and almost 40 for Salford. Manchester bought ADCs and Bristol Bs, the latter's large-for-the-time 5.96-litre engine providing all the necessary power and durability. Salford's purchases were more fragmented — ADC, Dennis, Leyland, Karrier and Guy, the last two makes following the short-lived fashion for six-wheel single-deckers.

It was a stressful time and there seems little doubt that this contributed to the sudden death of Henry Mattinson. In his place came perhaps the most famous of all general managers. Notable for his bow ties (a great patriot, he would on suitable occasions wear one formed from a Union Jack) Stuart Pilcher was born in Liverpool and trained with the Montreal Tramways. At the age

KEYDATES continued

1928 Jan – NWRCC joins express bus scheme
Jul – first full-size Crossley bus (VM 3675) on trial with MCT
Sep – SCT offices destroyed by fire in Blackfriars – Henry Mattinson dies suddenly
– MCT Birchfields Road depot opened

1929 – MCT tram fleet reaches peak of 953 cars
Jan – Stuart Pilcher becomes MCT general manager
– MCT bus garage annexes at Princess Road and Queens Road opened
Jul – MCT order for 15 AEC single-deckers overruled by city council
Aug – MCT order for AEC Regents for 53 tram conversion overruled by city council
Oct – SCT Weaste depot opens
Nov – MCT title changed from Tramways to Transport

▲ One of Salford's two Karrier WL6/1s flanked by the two Karrier CL6, all with Hall Lewis bodies, posed before delivery in 1927. Also delivered in that year were 10 more WL6, bodied by Massey. The Karriers were not suited to the speeds or distances of the express services, there are stories of Oldham's Karriers arriving at Gatley and having to have their glowing brakes cooled with water from a hosepipe.
Bray & Son, Holmfirth via Geoff Lumb

The Bristol B had a simple and rugged four-cylinder engine which at 5.96-litres was large for its time and was just what was needed for the express services. When Manchester's Leyland Tigers and Crossley Sixes were delivered in 1930, the 27 Bs were moved to busy inter-suburban service 19. This ran from Droylsden, through Fairfield, Gorton, Belle Vue and Levenshulme to West Didsbury, and was single-deck operated at the time. There were two route variations in Levenshulme and instead of a service number, buses showed 'E' (via Errwood Road) or 'B' (Burnage Lane). Fleetnumber 80 is in Parrs Wood yard — both batches had Bristol bodies but the second batch differed in having the 'Edinburgh' cut-away platform. Note also the 'running number' plate in the holder on the front emergency exit. *MCT*

Photographs of the Manchester ADCs bought simultaneously with the Bristol Bs are comparatively rare, and ones of the six with bodies built by Davidson of Trafford Park are even more so. Davidson built good bodies and expanded until it became a victim of the slump in 1929. Its early bodies had this rather curious 'floating' cab. This picture is of ADC 416D NF 7811 taken on an express journey during its first year in service in 1927. The oil-smoke emitting Daimler 'Silent Knight' sleeve-valve six-cylinder engine was only 3.5 litres swept-volume — small compared with the Bristol, it also proved less reliable. *Museum of Transport archive*

The first full-size Crossley bus — Eagle VM 3675, chassis number 90000 — in Droylsden on its first journey in service. Its body was built to Manchester's design by Davidson, Crossley adopting the design when Davidson ceased trading due to the slump. VM 3675 ran on hire to MCT from July to September 1928, when the corporation bought it. It ran unnumbered for a year and then became fleetnumber 38. *Crossley Motors via Ferry Bosman*

of 24 he became general manager at Aberdeen, he then managed the complex conversion of Edinburgh's cable trams to electrical power and in 1929 took over at Manchester. Having arranged the building of 38 new 'Pullman' trams (colloquially known to his intense displeasure as 'Pilchers'), almost his next act was to recommend the conversion of the single-deck 53 tram service to buses. The first major tram conversion in Europe, it set the scene for the next 20 years.

The City Council accepted this plan but his repeated recommendations for a fleet of AECs and Leylands were summarily overruled in favour of the local manufacturers. The Leyland contracts were allowed to stand, but those for AECs were cancelled and replaced by ones with Crossley Motors Ltd, which was based in the industrial suburb of Gorton. The reasons were sound — the lean years of the slump were in progress and the two Crossley companies employed a great many people in the city. So it was that, for the next 20 years, Manchester came to have a fleet which was virtually unique — for whilst Crossley Brothers Ltd was a large company, Crossley Motors Ltd was relatively small and, until the end of the war, some 90% of its bus production was for the city. This meant that, like London, the Corporation had, to all intents and purposes, its own bus builder. The decision was almost an excellent one — the Crossley chassis was fine, as was its petrol engine, and Crossley's coachwork was excellent. The firm's Achilles' heel was its diesel engines, which never matched the reliability or durability of those of AEC, Leyland and Gardner — and certainly not the larger units built by Crossley Brothers.

Salford did something equally unusual, buying Dennis Lance double-deckers in 1930 and 1932. In the following year general manager James Moffet died suddenly and in his place, the Tramways Committee appointed John William Blakemore, who had started with the Department as a points boy. Salford then bought what Stuart Pilcher had wanted — a fleet roughly composed of 50% AECs and 50% Leylands, and all should have been in good shape. However, it seems that Salford's bus overhaul and maintenance procedures were run on a somewhat ad hoc basis with no dedicated bus workshop or overhaul schedule. Buses were repaired as and when needed, with the work done amongst tramcars in line on the pits. By the start of the Second World War things in Salford would be badly awry.

The jointly operated express bus services caused a re-awakening of interest in some sort of joint transport board for all the local municipalities and a series of meetings was held, chaired by Stuart Pilcher. Named SELEC (South East Lancashire and East Cheshire), the group produced various reports during the 1930s but there was no real enthusiasm.

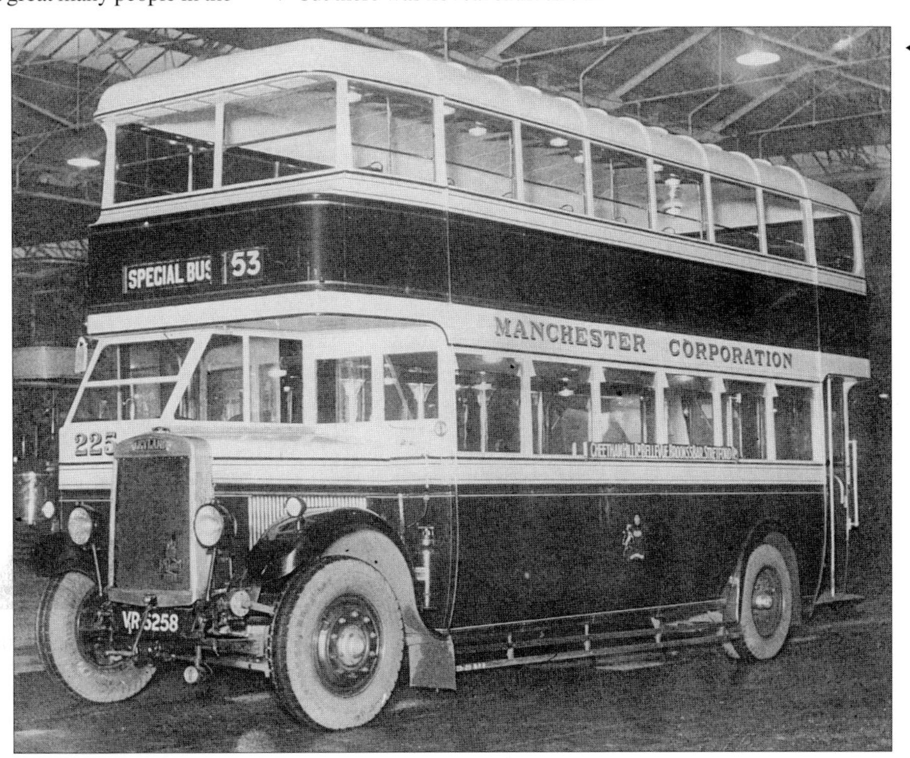

◄ Manchester bought 20 Crossley Condors and 40 TD1s for the 53 tram conversion, which was the first major tramway abandonment in Europe. The Condors were bodied by Brush, Arnold and Crossley and the TD1s by Short Brothers, Strachan and Brush. A superb night shot of the first of the Short Brothers-bodied batch, Leyland Titan TD1 225, in Queens Road depot. The date is February 1930, the bus just having been washed after arrival from Short's works at Rochester. Although superficially similar to the Leyland lowbridge body, Manchester specified the double upper-deck gangway layout. *MCT*

This is Salford 71 (BA 7676), a 1929 AEC 426 with Hall Lewis dual-entrance bodywork. The model before the Reliance, this chassis had the old four-cylinder engine, much as the S-type of 1922, and not the six-cylinder unit fitted to the Reliance. *SCT*

The express services are nicely captured in this picture of a 1930 Salford AEC Reliance in SHMD territory at the Greenfield Street, Hyde, terminus of service 8 to Bolton. Running every 12/15 minutes, the Reliance's place would be taken successively by a Lancashire United Leyland Tiger, a Manchester Crossley Six and a Bolton Leyland Tiger. There were some 40 express services, the network extending into Cheshire, Lancashire, Yorkshire and Derbyshire, covering the area bounded by Warrington, Wigan, Bolton, Rawtenstall, Bacup, Littleborough (Rochdale), Uppermill and Greenfield beyond Oldham, Mossley, Glossop, Hazel Grove, Poynton, Gatley and Altrincham. Operation involved the Manchester, Salford, Stockport, Ashton, SHMD, Oldham, Rochdale, Bury, Ramsbottom, Rawtenstall, Bolton and Leigh municipalities plus Lancashire United and North Western. Ribble co-operated and Burnley was also involved for a short time. *C. W. Heaps collection*

◄ Salford's Greengate terminus was a dark, damp and dismal tunnel beneath Exchange Station. Lancashire United Leyland-bodied Leyland Titan TD1 fleetnumber 30 (TF 3567), bound for Warrington, emerges from the gloom and passes a Salford AEC on the Weaste local service. The Warrington express service was jointly operated by Lancashire United and Salford but not Warrington Corporation, which was not a partner in the Co-ordinated Motor Bus Scheme. An express service worked by double-deckers was unusual — until the war the majority (later rebranded as 'limited stop') were single-deck worked. *SCT*

◄ Although it bought AEC single-deckers in 1929, Salford chose the unusual Dennis H for its 10 new double-deckers. In both cases Hall Lewis built the bodies, those on the double-decks being of lowbridge, double side-gangway layout. The driving position was set rather high, hence the awkward-looking windscreen layout. *SCT*

Stuart Pilcher never missed an opportunity to bring Manchester's fleet into the public eye and when Crossley Condor 249 was new in 1930, he arranged for it to take the British delegation to the International Transport Association Conference in Paris. Much photographed, including its journey on the deck of Captain Townsend's first cross-Channel ferry, it is seen here leaving Calais. People have come out of the shops to stare and a boy runs out of its path. The badges on the radiator are Crossley's royal warrants — granted for supplying cars to the King and Prince of Wales, the badges only appeared on the firm's buses. *MCT*

4. The Glorious Pilcher Years

Seventy years on, it is easy to forget that in the early 1930s, a bus had a petrol engine, did about four miles per gallon, had a body with a timber frame and a planned life of only seven or eight years. Impressed by the work on bus design and diesel engines being done by Messrs G. J. Rackham and C. B. Dicksee at AEC (Pilcher and Rackham shared a transatlantic background) and the resulting economy in fuel consumption (10-11 miles per gallon plus a much lower fuel price), in 1931 Stuart Pilcher took the bold step of adopting the diesel as standard. He was the first to do so.

The City Council was not going to allow purchases of AECs — or any more Leylands for a few years. This should have involved no risk, since Crossley Brothers' gas and oil engines had a formidable reputation for reliability and durability and it was reasonable to assume that these skills would transfer to its motor-making subsidiary. Practice proved somewhat different and Crossley's bus diesel engines were to have various weaknesses. Pre-war, this seems to have stemmed from a 1930 military contract to produce a diesel that was interchangeable with Crossley Motors' compact six-cylinder petrol engine — the result was a crankshaft and crankcase of insufficient strength to withstand the extra strains and stresses produced by a diesel engine. That apart, the Crossley engine worked as well as those of the other large bus manufacturers and Manchester led the way to general adoption of diesel buses. Exciting times indeed, as engineers from many other undertakings visited the Car Works and Parrs Wood, the Department's dedicated bus garage opened in 1926, to observe progress.

Bodywork came next on Stuart Pilcher's engineering agenda. In 1931 The Metropolitan-Cammell Carriage & Wagon Co Ltd ('Metro-Cammell') decided to add to its large and successful railway vehicle business by becoming a major supplier of bus bodies and to do so by using an all-steel body frame of standard design. It patented the frame and built 12 prototypes, of which Manchester took one (fleet number 390). The result was excellent and without further ado Stuart Pilcher adopted it, keeping the Council happy by arranging for Crossley to buy frames or frame kits from Metro-Cammell and complete them at Gorton. Interestingly, the flat sloping front that was a feature of the Metro-Cammell body was another AEC/Rackham design.

Known as 'The Standard', the body followed an established Manchester practice commenced on the tramcars and carried on in Stuart Pilcher's 'Piano-front' single- and double-deck bus body style, in that all the main panels, windows and parts were of standard design. Some 200 new Standards were delivered between 1933 and 1937 — and by careful manipulation of the politics, 15 were on Leyland chassis. By 1935 many of the timber-framed Piano-front bodies were ageing and they were

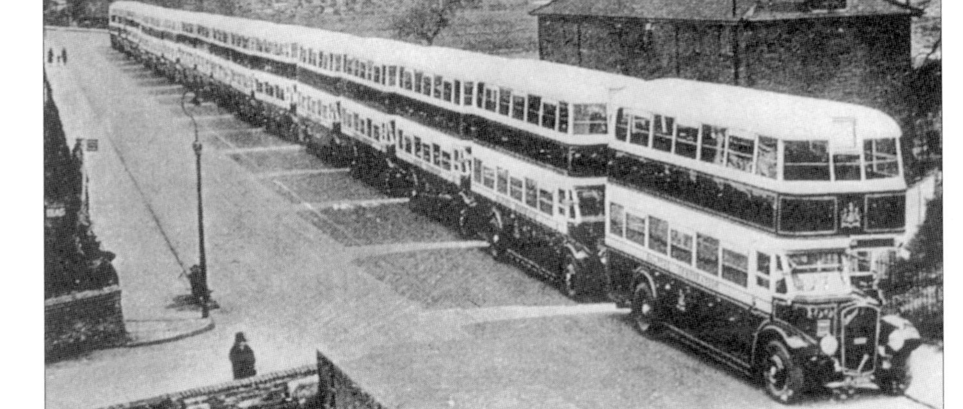

◄ A pre-delivery line-up of Salford's 18 Park Royal-bodied Dennis Lance IIs new in 1932, led by fleetnumber 100. The indicator layout was as unusual as the choice of chassis — a roof route number box and the destination box attached to the nearside canopy. *Dennis Brothers Ltd*

KEYDATES

1930 – MCT 53 tram converted to buses (first major tram conversion in Europe)
Jun – 39 express services in operation
Dec – MCT takes delivery of Gardner-engined Crossley

1931 – Police object to traffic congestion in city. Railways object to express buses
Jul – MCT decides all future buses will be diesel
Oct – Piccadilly Bus Station opens, start of enforced splitting of cross-city express services

continued

KEYDATES continued

1933 – J. S. D. Moffett dies suddenly, J. W. Blakemore appointed SCT general manager
– MCT bus route mileage 237 of which 106 is outside the city
Jul – MCT decides to standardise on metal-framed bodies
– Split of most Manchester /Salford cross-city tram services
– Salford introduces TIM ticket machines

1935 Mar – Swinton and Pendlebury trams converted, first major SCT abandonment
Apr – Manchester City Council raises trolleybus issue
May – City Council overrules diesels in favour of trolleybus on Ashton Old Road

continued

The shape of things to come. This picture, taken in Manchester's Princess Road garage in January 1933, has been used many times before but there is no other which so well captures the end of the timber-framed 'piano-front' era with Crossley-bodied Condors on the left and Hurst-Nelson ones on the right. At the end, facing the camera, is 390, one of Metro-Cammell's 12 prototypes of its new steel-framed body. Manchester immediately standardised on it, keeping local content by purchasing frames or frame kits from Metro-Cammell and having them finished by Crossley or the Car Works. *MCT*

replaced by new steel-framed Standard bodies. Thus the city quickly had a very modern, up to date looking and durable bus fleet with a life expectancy of 15 years instead of seven or eight. The first Standard, 390, arrived in November 1932, the last (546, by then 2546) was withdrawn late in 1953.

Salford also recognised a good thing and from 1934 most of its orders for bodywork went to Metro-Cammell. Salford chose to stay with the larger 8.8-litre engine for its pre-war AECs and one cannot help thinking that Stuart Pilcher must have cast the odd envious glance across the Irwell, coupled with dismay at the increasing lack of maintenance which the Salford bus and tram fleet was to receive as the 1930s progressed.

Next on the Pilcher schedule was appearance. In 1934 he told his team that he wanted 'something striking' for the city. The result of their work was the ultra-modern 'Streamliner' with its gracefully curved profiles, rounded window corners and stylish art deco paintwork whilst underneath was the durable Metro-Cammell or English Electric (and eventually Crossley) steel frame. The interior of the Streamliner was equally exuberant — most were trimmed in red, some were blue, others green and the early ones had alternate rows of seats in contrasting colours.

A total of 773 Streamliners was built, including 60 single-deckers that looked more like coaches than buses and 153 trolleybuses. Vastly successful, the first Streamliner (Crossley Mancunian 551) went into service in November 1936 and the last (Daimler COG5 1266, by then 4266) was withdrawn some 26 years later, in September 1962 — and bear in mind that those 26 years included the Second World War.

Whilst all this exciting engineering work was going on, the trams were progressively being replaced by buses, a new town was built at Wythenshawe with services needing over 100 buses and the other bus services were expanded. Not that all was rosy. A combination of railway company pressure and the Chief Constable's objections to traffic congestion in Market Street caused by the tramcars and buses had led to the splitting of the cross-city express bus services commencing in 1930 and their termination in the new Piccadilly Bus Station for services to the east and south, or Cannon Street (and later Stevenson Square) for

After buying Dennis, Salford went to AEC and Leyland for its buses and in 1934 bought 10 Leyland Titan TD3s, five of which had diesel engines and Metro-Cammell steel-framed bodies. The other five were petrol engined and had timber-framed Massey bodies, styled to be of similar appearance to the 1932 Lances. This is 28 (RJ 3008) when newly delivered. The destination indicator layout was the same as that of contemporary Manchester vehicles. *SCT*

Salford bought two batches of Crossley Mancunians — four in 1934 and five in 1938. Two of the 1934 batch had Massey bodies, similar to that on Leyland 28 (*above right*); the other two (114/5) had Metro-Cammell bodies to Manchester's design and were more or less identical to Manchester's 501-520. This picture shows 115 in autumn 1949 after sale for use as a transport café in Weaste. *R. L. Wilson*

Outside the Wellington Hotel, Didsbury, Manchester's 1937 Metro-Cammell/Crossley-bodied Crossley Mancunian 'Standard' 2595 and Leyland-bodied Leyland Titan TD5 'Streamliner' 3812 turning from Barlow Moor Road into Wilmslow Road. The lady cyclist is about to get a few lungfuls of 2595's exhaust. Although lacking the flamboyance of the Streamliner, the Standard-bodied Mancunians had a purposeful down-to-earth look about them, which seemed very appropriate for a city bus. *N. R. Knight*

When Salford bought its AEC Regents, Stuart Pilcher must have looked on enviously, wishing that the Manchester City Council was not swayed by local influences. Repainted in the postwar green livery, 1935 Metro-Cammell-bodied AEC Regent 123 (RJ 3522) is in Victoria Bus Station. The steps lead to Victoria Bridge Street, terminus of several other Salford services. The bus had an 8.8-litre engine, recognisable by the protruding radiator. Although AEC's 7.7-litre engine, introduced in 1936, became the more popular choice, Salford continued to specify the larger unit. *Roy Marshall*

The last of 25 Leyland Titans delivered to Salford in 1936 was fleetnumber 152 (RJ 6625). From 1934 to 1940, Salford's orders were split between AEC and Leyland and in 1936 there were 10 AEC Regents and 25 Leyland Titans. The Regents and 20 of the Titans, including 152, had all-metal Metro-Cammell bodies. General manager Blakemore continued to buy a few timber-framed Massey bodies (five this year) and a mixture of Leylands with crash gearboxes (15) and torque-converter transmission (10). *SCT*

Salford single-deck purchases of the 1930s were mainly English Electric-bodied AEC Regals but in 1937 three Leyland Tigers with Massey bodies were purchased — this picture is of fleetnumber 7 (RJ 7005). In addition to services needing single-deckers because of low bridges or narrow roads, before the war many of the limited stop services in both cities were single-deck operated. *SCT*

Salford 159 (RJ 6632), a 1936 AEC Regent with a Metro-Cammell body in Victoria Bridge Street. Comparing the bodywork detail of this bus with the ones of the Salford and Manchester Crossleys shows clearly how the Manchester Standard design differed in subtle details from Metro-Cammell's own standard — for example, in having no rain shields above the upper-deck windows and a slightly more rounded rear dome. Behind 159 is Salford 1928 Dennis E fleetnumber 53. *SCT via P. Greaves collection*

services to the north, with Victoria Bridge Street and Greengate for Salford's buses and the isolated Lower Mosley Street for long distance services.

More trouble from the City Council was to come for the Manchester manager in the shape of the trolleybus. In addition to his duties as general manager, Stuart Pilcher was a prolific writer of papers and wrote regularly for the respected industry magazine *Bus & Coach*. As early as 1932 he had set out his views on trolleybuses in *Bus & Coach*, showing that they cost more to build and operate than diesels. In 1935, influenced by London's decision to build a trolleybus network, some members of the City Council began to lobby for trolleybuses. Whilst a perfect gentleman and always extremely courteous to everyone whosoever they were, Stuart Pilcher was also very forceful and dedicated to his goals, and did not take kindly to inexperienced lay people, such as councillors, giving operational or technical advice to industry professionals. The result was war.

After much lobbying by the pro-trolleybus group, including placing of advertisements in the local papers and countered by almost two years' delaying tactics on Stuart Pilcher's part, the first battle was lost. The City Council ordered that the Ashton New Road and Ashton Old Road tramcars be converted to trolleybuses and a garage for them built in Rochdale Road, just north of Miller Street. On 1 March 1938, the trolleybus system opened. Dislike them he might but Stuart Pilcher did his usual first-class job and gave the city a superb system with the most modern vehicles in the country — Streamliners of course — and excellent overhead wiring. The network grew to include the Ashton-Haughton Green and Greenheys-Miller Street services, although the war caused postponement of plans to convert the Hyde Road trams. Instead the trolleybuses and equipment bought for it were used to convert the busy Moston (via Rochdale Road and Oldham Road) bus services, thus saving precious diesel fuel, and the Hyde service was eventually converted after the war.

Stuart Pilcher handled the second battle, conversion of all the remaining tram services, with more subtlety. After careful and lengthy reports, perilously close voting, various convenient traffic jams and use of councillors to alter vehicle orders, the day was won and conversion of the remaining trams was agreed. The timescale was 18 months fro February 1939 and something like 400 new Streamliners were needed. Building this quantity in such a short timescale was beyond Crossley's peacetime capacity and the firm was increasingly involved in military vehicle production. By cleverly turning the City Council's opposition to advantage, Stuart Pilcher contrived that the City Council altered the orders to be divided more or less equally between Crossley, Leyland and Daimler, the latter using the locally-made Gardner engine, with Leyland and English Electric supplying bodies in addition to the usual Metro-Cammell Crossley build. The project was almost completed when war intervened and deliveries of vehicles were stopped. All the Leylands were delivered but the bombing of Daimler's factory in Coventry meant that 43 of the 116 Daimler chassis did not arrive and Crossley bus production stopped with 71 complete vehicles owed. Both orders were completed after the war.

Pressing on with its own tram replacement, Salford also placed large orders in the years before the war, receiving 105 new buses in 1938-1940, bringing its bus fleet total to 225. In 1941 47% of Salford's fleet was under three years-old.

KEYDATES continued

1936 Jul – City Council enforces order for trolleybuses
– MCT TIM ticket machines introduced at Princess Road
Oct – first MCT Streamliners completed

1937 – Split of remaining cross-Manchester-Salford tram journeys
6 Dec – SCT's Victoria Bus Station opens

1938 Mar – MCT Rochdale Road Garage opened, trolleybus system opened
– MCT Queens Road garage becomes all bus

1939 Feb – MCT decision to scrap rest of trams within 18 months, large orders for buses
– MCT Princess Road garage becomes all bus
– MCT Northenden garage opened part completed

◂ Streamlined luxury. Manchester's first airport coach was this nice little one-off Crossley Delta, fleetnumber 6 (BVU 98), new in November 1935. Noted for the quality of their finish, the Gorton staff took even more care with the coachwork which was very much in the streamline mode appropriate for the then avant garde world of air travel. Unlike the later airport coaches which were painted blue, the Delta was finished in red and white. *MCT*

▲ Kingsway ran past Manchester's Parrs Wood garage at a slightly higher level than the garage yard and provided an excellent location for photography. Taken on 16 April 1950 this picture shows Crossley Condors, 2333, 2343, 2347 and Mancunian 2439. All had been rebodied with Metro-Cammell/Crossley 'Standard' bodies in 1937. A Leyland Tiger TS8 Streamliner single-decker is next to 2439 and behind the four buses the yard contains a variety of Standards and Streamliners plus a single postwar PD1. *C. W. Heaps*

A cold, wet November day in 1936 with Manchester's first Streamliner, 551, newly delivered from Crossley's Gorton works. The bus is posed near Parrs Wood garage, accompanied by the Department's 'fog pilot' vehicles — four motor cycles and a Ford van which were used to guide convoys of buses in the smoke-laden 'pea soup' winter fogs. The picture shows the first Streamliner livery with the horizontal flash on the upper-deck sides, note also the 'Crossley Coachwork' transfer at the front corner of the cab. The elegant flowing lines and art deco paintwork were a revolution in bus design, for which the norm of the time was 'everything square' with elaborate lining out in gold. *MCT* ▶

The Leyland body adapted well to the outlines of the Streamliner and such was the buying power of Manchester that Leyland was more than willing to make the various styling and finishing changes. Crossley Mancunian 729 was sent to Leyland to provide guidance. Leyland's standard frame needed only small modifications, compared with the Metro-Cammell/Crossley the resulting front profile was slightly more upright, the cab was pure Leyland but otherwise, as this picture shows, everything else was 'Streamliner' and the result was a very elegant vehicle. This is no. 804, the second of a batch of 12, at Leyland's works in November 1938. *Leyland Motors via Ian Allan library* ▼

◀ A picture of new Crossley Mancunian 746 outside the portico of the Manchester Central Reference Library in December 1938, taken to show off its Car Works body, built as usual on a Metro-Cammell steel frame. The bus also had the first Crossley synchromesh gearbox. The picture shows the third and final version of the streamline livery with the upper-deck swoop but omitting the small swoop behind the lower-deck offside wheels. The indicators are badly set and had the bus been in service, the Piccadilly or Albert Square inspector would have had something to say to the crew. *MCT*

▲ Towards the end of the 1930s Manchester still had some lowbridge timber-framed bodies on Crossley Condor chassis and was also discovering problems with the Accles & Pollock frames on vehicles 436-465. It therefore decided to build 80 'interim life' bodies in the Car Works. This shorter life enabled the use of timber frames, providing employment for the Car Works bodybuilders who had a reducing tramcar workload. Known as the 'Car Works Composite', the body used standard parts and the result was a curious mixture of the Standard and the Streamliner. War intervened and only 26 were built. This is Condor 408 photographed in 1950 at Old Trafford en route to Trafford Park for the evening rush hour. *R. L. Wilson*

With their half canopy, raised rear window line and streamline markings, Manchester's 40 Leyland Tiger TS8 single-deck Streamliners and their 20 Crossley counterparts, new in 1937 and 1938, looked more like coaches than service buses. During the war most were fitted out for easy conversion to ambulances should they be needed, carrying a set of stretchers in a canvas covered frame which can be seen on the platform of fleetnumber 60 in this picture. The roofs were painted grey as a wartime measure to make them less visible to the Luftwaffe. The second bus is fleetnumber 61. *MCT* ▶

Manchester (Ringway) Airport was soon back in business after the war and experienced rapid growth. The little Crossley Delta was replaced by Leyland Tiger TS8s which were rebuilt as coaches, using the existing body frames. Eight were so treated by a variety of coachbuilders over the period 1946 to 1950. This is fleetnumber 97, one of two rebuilt in 1950 by County Motors of Leigh to 30-seat front-entrance coaches. Finished in dark blue and white with new yet well-matched polished trim and carefully maintained at Parrs Wood, they looked very smart. *R. L. Wilson*
▼

◀ When the Dane Bank estate was built in Denton a shuttle service was introduced to Reddish, connecting with the trunk services to Manchester and Stockport. It was decided that this would be one-man-operated and Manchester took the unusual route of converting one of the Leyland Tiger TS8s to normal control. Passengers paid the flat fare of one penny into a simple farebox. Fleetnumber 71 on one of its first days in service in 1949. *R. L. Wilson*

Salford's AEC single-deckers somehow seemed unusual and exotic. This is 171, one of five Regals with Preston-built English Electric bodies, supplied in late 1937. Three similar buses had been delivered earlier in the year and five more followed in 1939. All had 8.8-litre engines. *Roy Marshall*

In Greengate, just outside the back end of the arches, Salford 196 (RJ 8740), a 1938 Metro-Cammell-bodied Leyland Titan TD5c, waits to work a racecourse special in 1948. It has just been overhauled, during which its torque converter was replaced by a conventional gearbox. Behind is another bus from the same batch, still in red and brown wartime livery. *Roy Marshall*

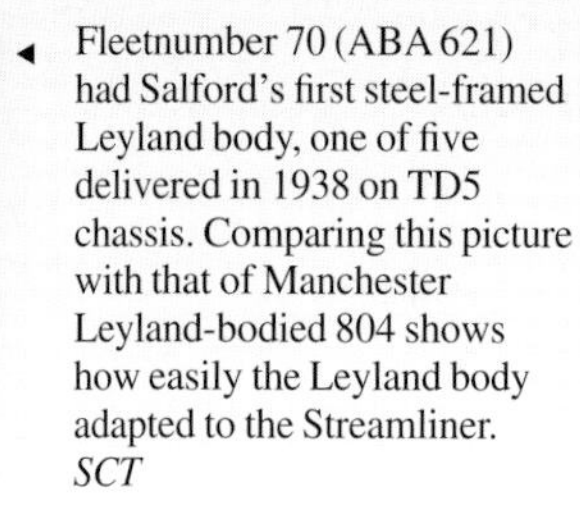

Fleetnumber 70 (ABA 621) had Salford's first steel-framed Leyland body, one of five delivered in 1938 on TD5 chassis. Comparing this picture with that of Manchester Leyland-bodied 804 shows how easily the Leyland body adapted to the Streamliner. *SCT*

The new green and primrose paint gleams on the Park Royal bodywork of 1938 AEC Regent 49 in Queens Drive, Sedgeley Park. Another example of Charles Baroth's pride in his fleet can be seen in the 'Salford City Transport' badge on the radiator. From 1946 makers' radiator nameplates were removed from buses as they were repainted or delivered new and replaced by these badges. *C. W. Heaps collection*

▲
Salford 232, one of five Leyland-bodied TD5s new in 1940, in Prestwich on a short working of the long, inter-suburban service 6 from Radcliffe to Eccles. *C. W. Heaps collection*

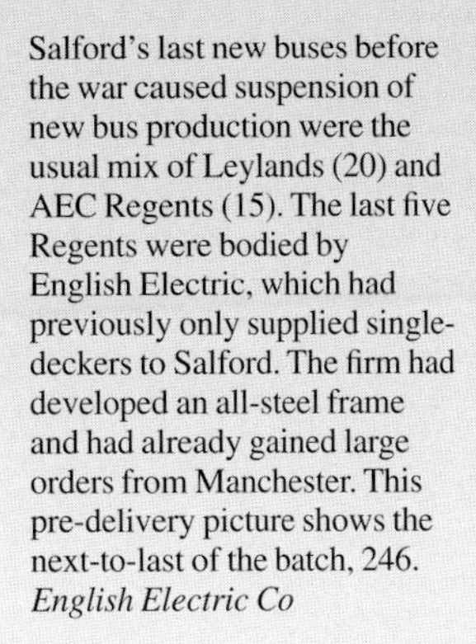

Salford's last new buses before the war caused suspension of new bus production were the usual mix of Leylands (20) and AEC Regents (15). The last five Regents were bodied by English Electric, which had previously only supplied single-deckers to Salford. The firm had developed an all-steel frame and had already gained large orders from Manchester. This pre-delivery picture shows the next-to-last of the batch, 246. *English Electric Co* ▶

◀ Brand new Crossley four-wheel trolleybus 1016 turning from Aytoun Street to come onto the Ashton/Stalybridge stand for services 28 and 29 in 1938. The trolleybus body design had a subtle difference from the diesel Streamliners, having an inward curving lower rear profile, which better balanced the full front end, whereas the diesel Streamliner body was slightly flared outwards.
P. G. Greaves collection

Manchester's six-wheeled Leyland TTB4 trolleybus 1068, new in 1938, turns from Aytoun Street to pull onto the 218/219 terminus at the top of Portland Street, Piccadilly. Apart from having no wheel trims, the six-wheel Crossleys, 1050-1061, looked exactly the same.
R. L. Wilson
▼

5. Wartime

KEYDATES

1940-5 – MCT loans over 100 buses to other operators

1940 – SCT tram fleet down to 61 cars
– MCT Moston trolleybus conversions to save fuel

1941 – SCT bus fleet slips into serious decline
– AEC RT19 demonstrates to MCT (influences the Crossley DD42)

1942 – MCT Northenden garage completed, most of it taken for aircraft production

The wartime period can be summarised in a dozen words — Manchester did more than its bit and Salford got into a mess. With its modern diesel fleet and fine new trolleybus system, Manchester was able to reinstate some tram services, postpone further conversions and loan over 100 buses, including the 40 Leyland TD1s which had been rebodied with Standard bodies, to others in need. Grey replaced white in the livery when buses needed repainting — the grey and red scheme looked quite smart — and all bus roofs were painted grey. The new Northenden garage, built to house the growing fleet of buses which served Wythenshawe, was commandeered for production of war material before the Department could occupy all of it, along with part of Parrs Wood and a temporary parking area was arranged in Wythenshawe Park.

At Salford, in spite of having a fleet as modern as that of Manchester and being able to delay tram conversions, general manager Blakemore seems to have been totally out of his depth. Almost new Titans and Regents lay around awaiting repairs, often trapped on the pits behind broken down trams or other defunct buses. In 1941 the Ministry of War Transport investigated this situation, discovering that of a fleet of 225 buses, 68 were out of service and although only 165 were required for normal operations there were insufficient serviceable buses to meet this need. The Ministry threatened to take away the surplus vehicles for repair and use elsewhere but there was only a token gesture of sending two 1939 Leyland-bodied TD5s to Coventry in 1941 to assist after the blitz. The situation did not improve. Instead, extra seats were fitted into the upper-deck of many buses to make the 48-seaters into 52 or 54-seaters — any spare from any unserviceable bus was used whether it matched or not, giving the fleet an even more neglected look.

In mid-1943 with no improvement achieved, the Salford management was summoned to a meeting at the Ministry in London where they were told to adopt a regular docking and overhaul procedure on a mileage basis, that engines should be overhauled every 100,000 miles, that vehicles should receive a general overhaul every two years and that the maintenance section must be organised. It seems quite incredible that such practices were not in place and it compared dreadfully with Manchester's sophisticated system, which had been in operation since 1930. There was little progress; the Ministry had another try in 1944 but things did not improve.

When the war ended Salford's bus and tram fleet was in a terrible state — some buses were faded red and white, others were red and brown, some were grey or grey and white, and the odd one was brown all over. Most were battered and many had bits missing. Buses carried two fleetnumbers, the main one and also a 'garage fleetnumber' prefixed C for Central (Frederick Road) and W for Weaste — allocated in a similarly chaotic manner to the fleet numbers, their purpose was obscure. On the lower front nearside panel buses also carried a large number in a

▸ Manchester buses repainted during the war were finished in red and grey, and many people thought the result looked quite smart. This summer 1947 picture shows 1934 Crossley Mancunian 'Standard' 504 in Westinghouse Road outside the large peak-hour bus terminus close to Metropolitan Vickers' Main Gate. Several Manchester Streamliners can be seen in the background of this picture. Serving Trafford Park was a mammoth task. Over 450 Manchester and Salford buses worked the peak-hour journeys to and from Trafford Park; even in the car-dominated 1960s the figure was still 290.
P. Greaves collection

◄ This picture of Victoria Bus Station on a cold dark winter's evening in 1945 captures the dreadful state into which the Salford fleet had deteriorated. The AEC Regent on the 85 is battered, its nearside headlamp lacks a glass and its bonnet side is loose, whilst 1937 Regent 182 with its back to the camera lacks a rear destination blind and is painted red and brown but has its fleet number in a grey circle. The latter's 'garage' fleet number (C51) can be seen above the staircase window. In front is another red and brown bus but its red paint was left untouched when the brown was applied, evidenced by the reflection from the gold lining-out. *Museum of Transport archive/Kay*

circle. This was the number of the longest service which the bus was considered fit to operate — for example, '26' meant that the bus was considered capable of running to Leigh and back without breaking down. The trams were even worse. It was all terribly sad.

Perhaps the only good outcome was that Salford placed sizeable orders for new buses, hedging its bets on delivery by going for a mixture — 16 Crossley DD42, 15 AEC Regent III and 18 Leyland PD1, all with Metro-Cammell bodies, plus 17 Leyland-bodied PD1s. General Manager Blakemore also agreed to Stuart Pilcher's 1945 proposal to abandon the Deansgate tram tracks in 1947 — these were used by the remaining Salford tram services and this meant converting them all to buses. It was a risky plan.

In 1946 both general managers were due to retire. The government asked Manchester to release Stuart Pilcher early, as they wished him to take up the prestigious post of West Midlands Traffic Commissioner, to which Manchester agreed. He placed orders for no less than 877 new buses — 344 Crossleys (including 54 trolleybuses and the 71 buses owed from prewar orders), 233 Daimlers (including the 43 owed from prewar) and 300 Leylands. He also instituted the 'thousands' fleet numbering system (1-199 single-deckers, 1000-series trolleybuses, 2000-series Crossleys, 3000-series Leylands, 4000-series Daimlers). That done, Stuart Pilcher said goodbye to his staff at a huge party, held at Belle Vue and organised by the Engineering Department, and departed to the West Midlands. In 1943 the king had awarded him the CBE for his services to transport.

His successor, Albert Neal BSc (Eng), AMIEE, MInstT was currently deputy at Pilcher's old command at Edinburgh. A graduate of London University, he had started his career in industry with English Electric whence he had been recruited by Stuart Pilcher as one of the many bright young engineers and traffic staff who were trained at Manchester. Albert Neal had moved to Edinburgh before the war to gain experience (it is generally assumed he was being 'groomed' by Stuart Pilcher)

and there would be little change of direction in Manchester, although in personality he was quite the opposite of the extroverted Stuart Pilcher. A very private man, to many people Albert Neal seemed cold and aloof, for his task of managing through ever decreasing passenger numbers and rising costs was not easy. However, the few who knew him well found a warm and caring person, as instanced by the following vignette. Manchester was always helpful towards enthusiasts, requests being handled by the publicity department, but when a severely disabled young bus enthusiast who lived hundreds of miles from the city wrote for a fleet list, Albert Neal wrote a personal letter — and remembered to do so every year thereafter. A kind and thoughtful man.

Another example of the sorry state of the Salford fleet at the end of the war. Metro-Cammell-bodied AEC Regent 201 (ABA 633) is in the red and brown livery and carries the various numbers with which the Salford fleet was adorned during the war. The garage fleet number is C20 (C was for Central garage, the name for Frederick Road) but the most bizarre item is the number 26 in the circle, which indicated that the bus was considered fit to work service 26 (Leigh). The picture was taken in 1948, by which time Charles Baroth was in full control and there would have been no question of anything so disreputable-looking being used in service — the bus was on driver training duties. *R. L. Wilson*

A variety of liveries. Salford Leyland Titan TD5 222, new in 1940, is brown and red. It has already had mechanical attention, evidenced by a new radiator cowl and headlamps in readiness for its coming repaint into the green livery. Behind is 1937 AEC Regent 184, another wartime repaint but this time in grey and white, to the right is another Regent that has already been repainted green. All three had Metro-Cammell bodies.
Roy Marshall

By contrast John William Blakemore must have been extremely thankful when his last day in office came. The Salford Transport Committee looked round for a successor. Although Salford was the third largest municipal fleet in Lancashire the job was not over-attractive given the dreadful state of its vehicles, which was openly said to be the worst of any in the kingdom. Someone of exceptional ability and determination was needed.

The committee found him. Charles W. Baroth, MInstT was currently in charge at Newport Corporation Transport and if Manchester's glory days were to dim a little under Albert Neal, Salford was about to experience a most glorious dawn.

◄ Almost at the end of its life, repainted all-red and long since fitted with a Leyland 8.6-litre engine and gearbox, Crossley's postwar prototype DD42 (Manchester 2960) passes Mauldeth Road as it makes its way along a misty Wilmslow Road into the city from Gatley on the 162x service on 20 February 1963. It was withdrawn in June of that year and sold for scrap. *Ian Allan library (R. G. Harman)*

◄ Forty three of Manchester's 1939/40 orders for 116 Daimler COG5 chassis were not delivered, due to the bombing of Daimler's Coventry works, and the chassis order was fulfilled in 1945 with Daimler CWA6s 4200-4242. All the English Electric bodies intended for the COGs were delivered, the Department used some itself and sold the remainder to Birmingham Corporation; the bodies for the CWA6s were built by Brush. This is 4240 in Parker Street in the summer of 1948. As with many utility bodies, the timber used for the framing was 'green' and deteriorated quickly. The corporation contemplated rebodying them and making a larger batch by buying some ex-London CWA6s but after investigation the 43 buses were sold for scrap in 1951/2. *R. L. Wilson*

6. Glory Days in Salford

KEYDATES

1946 – MCT 'thousands' fleet numbering scheme introduced
– MCT orders 877 Leyland, Daimler and Crossley buses
Jun – Stuart Pilcher asked by government to become Chairman of West Midlands TC
Aug – C. W. Baroth becomes SCT general manager
Sep – A. F. Neal becomes MCT general manager
– SCT green/cream livery with silver roof introduced

1947 Feb – SCT order for 210 Daimler CVG6
31 Mar – last SCT tram
– MCT Princess Road trams abandoned

1948 – MCT Kingsway trams abandoned
Feb – MCT livery revised, red roof for 8ft, grey roof for 7ft 6in

1949 10 Jan – last MCT tram

1950 – Hyde (Gee Cross) trolleybus starts
– MCT external side advertising introduced
– MCT introduces Ultimate ticket machines

Charles Baroth very quickly achieved a remarkable transformation. A strict maintenance code, based on prevention rather than cure, was introduced along with a rigid mileage-based docking system. This was backed up by high quality specifications for new vehicles. Attention to detail such as use of low sulphur diesel fuel (it was available in the 1940s, 1950s and 1960s) and a high quality engine oil, and making drivers use first gear when starting, in place of the then usual practice of starting in second, ensured that the Gardner engines would complete half a million miles without major attention.

The livery was changed to a smart dark green and primrose with silver roof — the choice was in part to distinguish Salford buses from those of Manchester. Interestingly, Stuart Pilcher's Pullman trams had had silver roofs and he had experimented with silver roofs on a few buses in 1945. The old ornate shaded gold lettering was replaced by a crisp modern typeface and the undertaking's name changed to Salford City Transport. Street furniture received attention, with new bus stop flags, signs and new bus shelters bearing a smartly painted green board with the undertaking's name in gold. The chaotic gap filling fleet numbering system was changed to a straight sequence for new buses.

Within 12 months more than 40% of the fleet was repainted into the new livery (including Metro-Cammell repainting the first of the new buses before delivery), 24 unserviceable buses had been fully overhauled and were back in use, and 10 Leyland Titan TD3 and TD4 chassis were being prepared to go to Burlingham for new bodies.

The North West was heavily industrialised and Salford had one of the highest atmospheric sulphur contents in the country, which influenced the new schedule of a complete vehicle repaint every two to two-and-a-half years. From 1953, to keep the fleet well groomed, the 'cap and gown' programme was introduced. Under this, each April the Salford paint shop ceased full repaints for a month and at least two thirds of the fleet would be taken in and smartened — roofs, wheels, mudguards were repainted, with attention to other areas as necessary.

These high standards applied to the whole fleet so that any bus, old or new, was capable of, and smart enough for a full day's duty on a heavily trafficked trunk route. And they would be expected to do just that when substitutes were needed for any unwashed buses which the general manager had noticed on his way to work ('Doesn't anybody ever wash this fleet?').

Bearing in mind the underlying organisation, culture and staff changes which all this required, the transformation was amazing. One does not achieve great things on one's own and, as had Stuart Pilcher, Charles Baroth surrounded himself with a talented team. There can be no better measure of this than the fact that five of his staff moved directly from Salford into general managers' posts — J. C. Franklin (Rochdale and Blackpool), F. Thorp (Bury and Newport), W. Wilson (Stockton), R. Palmer (Portsmouth) and, probably best known of all, Ronald Cox who moved to Rochdale, Bournemouth, Edinburgh and then became Director General of Greater Glasgow PTE.

Although much of Salford's prewar fleet had Metro-Cammell steel-framed bodies, there was an immense backlog of overhaul work and, although some bodies were overhauled by outside contractors, including Metro-Cammell and Samlesbury, the most cost effective solution was to replace the prewar buses as soon as practicable. New buses, especially bodies, were in short supply until 1949 and orders were placed for 210 Daimler CVG6, 195 with Metro-Cammell bodies and 15 with Burlingham single-deck bodies. With that size of order it was possible to specify many particular features and the Metro-Cammell bodies incorporated the straight staircase and large platform developed at Birmingham Corporation (Charles Baroth had worked for Midland Red in that city earlier in his career). Besides being particularly safe for passengers, a benefit of this layout was that in a rear-end collision the rear platform would fold into the body, avoiding expensive damage to the staircase. This was important — with the area's damp, smoky atmosphere of the time, icy roads and black ice were particularly prevalent in winter. For the same reasons, Manchester specified a suspended platform, whereby the platform is cantilevered out from the body and not supported on a chassis extension.

In the short term there remained the problem of the trams and the agreement made for Deansgate. Having little sympathy for Salford's self-inflicted plight and sufficient new buses to withdraw its own trams on Deansgate, an unsympathetic Manchester declined to alter the plan and offered to loan Salford some elderly Crossleys and lowbridge Leyland TD1s. Quite how this offer was worded is lost in the mists of time, but the result was a further deterioration in relations between the two transport departments. Instead, Charles Baroth bought or hired 20 second-hand buses, including Leylands and AECs from Wallasey, and the trams were gone. The old buses did not have to last long — in February 1947 the new Leyland PD1s, Crossleys and AEC Regents began to arrive. They were supplemented by 30 more Leyland-bodied PD1s, which Leyland offered as a result of the cancellation of an export order, and eight Metro-Cammell-bodied Daimler CVD6s which had been ordered by Chester but which were surplus to its needs — such over-ordering in the postwar scramble was not unusual.

The 30 Leylands were offered as PD2s with the 9.8-litre engine but Salford (like Manchester) decided to have the smaller 7.4-litre unit, believing that a small engine working hard gave better fuel economy. Over the years the larger engines proved much more durable and the consequent lower maintenance costs offset the fuel saving. Use of the smaller engine by both cities surprised Leyland, which had allocated a code (PD2/6) for Manchester's specification in anticipation, but it was 1951 before Manchester's first PD2 arrived.

That the hiring incident did nothing to improve cross-Irwell relations is evidenced by the following story. In the very cold winter of 1947 Manchester

◄◄ The first Salford Leyland PD1s were in build at Metro-Cammell when Charles Baroth was appointed and the first few had already been finished in red livery with 'gap filling' fleet numbers. Metro-Cammell took the usual maker's pictures including this one of what would have been fleetnumber 14 with registration number BRJ 903. However, before they were delivered in 1947, the new general manager decided to arrange fleet and registration numbers in sequence, and also had any completed vehicles repainted into the new green livery. This bus became 279 with registration number BRJ 933, registration number BRJ 903 being re-allocated to Crossley 249. *SCT*

◄ During the 1948/9 financial year, 10 Salford Leyland TD3 and TD4 Titans were fitted with new timber-framed bodies by Burlingham and renumbered 101-110. This picture shows 110 (RJ 3004) about to pull away from Worsley Court House with a full load of passengers. Built to a pre-war design, the bodies were similar to those supplied contemporaneously to Ribble for similar reconditioned chassis. An odd feature of Burlingham's design is shown in the picture — the cab door was hinged at the rear, a somewhat dangerous feature. *C. W. Heaps collection*

Inbound on Service 22 from Prestwich to Victoria in Bury New Road, Sedgeley Park, Prestwich on a 1950s Saturday is Metro-Cammell-bodied Crossley DD42/3 fleetnumber 259. The 22 was a short working on the 24 (Whitefield) with peak-hour journeys only on weekdays but a 10-13min service on Saturday.
C. W. Heaps

experienced problems starting its new Crossleys' HOE7 engines with their troublesome, asthmatic cylinder head. A Fordson tractor was therefore stationed in Piccadilly Bus Station, fitted with a front buffer made from bus seat squabs, it could be called up to give a gentle shove to awaken a reluctant HOE7. *The Manchester Evening News* discovered this and ran a rather unkind story with a picture, naming the little tractor the 'Bus Push'. Charles Baroth had the article framed and it sat on the office mantelpiece for many years.

In fact, only a few months earlier something very similar was to be found in Salford. Visiting Victoria Bus Station for the first time in 1946, the new General Manager spotted an old Dennis double-decker, converted to a van and displaying the word 'SERVICE' in large capitals. 'And just what kind of service does that offer?' he enquired and by way of reply was shown a large heavy towing chain that lived therein. 'No bus which bears my name, let alone that of the City of Salford, and which requires a device like that to move it, shall henceforth ever be allowed to leave the garage' he declared. The chain was despatched at once to Frederick Road, never to emerge again.

In a matter of a few months it was clear to the staff that Salford's buses were something to be proud of and for the next 20-odd years they were not to be seen to fail in public. If one did, the instructions were that if possible the crew should park it neatly ('push it if necessary'), preferably in a side street, with its indicators set to PRIVATE as if it were a school bus. It would then be recovered after dark by Salford's spotless ex-WD AEC Matador. Said to have seen war service at Narvik in 1940, its peacetime duty was soon confined to leading the Mayor of Salford's Annual Carnival Parade.

Staff culture changed too. In their last days the Salford trams were utterly decrepit and crews would seek any reason to fail one in service, the thinking being that Frederick Road was unlikely to have a serviceable replacement. Spare buses were in equally short supply and the hoped-for outcome was the crew's being stood down. The new General Manager's response was to park a tram in a very visible spot just inside Frederick Road's archway entrance, apparently ready to be exchanged at a moment's notice for any faulty car. Nothing was said, no memos were issued — they weren't necessary.

Another tale, probably apocryphal, concerns the 15 (Piccadilly-Worsley) service, remnant of the Guide Bridge-Worsley express that had been split in 1939 when the Guide Bridge portion became Manchester trolleybus 29. The truncated 15 was operated

by Salford and its Piccadilly terminus was at the top of Portland Street, in direct line of view from the window of Albert Neal's office at 55 Piccadilly. In the years to come, when his own fleet was being criticised by the City Council, the first thing he would see from his window was one of Charles Baroth's splendid Daimlers. The story is that the Salford general manager successfully resisted Manchester's attempts to move the 15's terminus. The Piccadilly gyratory system got it in the 1960s, the terminus moving into Piccadilly Bus Station where its new stand, probably by chance, was near to Mosley Street and as far away from 55 Piccadilly as it could be. Salford subsequently allocated its Atlanteans and Fleetlines to the service, as if to emphasise that its fleet was thoroughly up-to-date.

Manchester received scores of new buses in 1948 and 1949, all with Stuart Pilcher's final special design of body of which there was a total of 710. Still with a vestige of the Streamliner with the dip in its front upper-deck windows and the curved rear side windows, it also featured a 'suspended' platform. In Manchester's case the line of the two rear-most windows on both decks was raised to allow extra strengthening, giving an additional visual feature. Crossley had developed its own all-steel frame and the orders were for complete bodies from Crossley and Metro-Cammell plus 50 from Brush. Such was the preciseness of the specification that it was hard to detect any difference between them — there was a small difference in the line of the drip moulding aft of the side upper-deck windows and on the rear dome but that was about all. The first of the 7ft 6in postwar Crossleys had a single cream streamline swoop on the lower panels but this was given up before the batch was complete. Crossley 2028 was displayed at the 1948 Commercial Motor Show in an updated livery of red with a cream band above the lower-deck windows and around the upper-deck ones, which was adopted from bus 2056, 3100 and 4000-4049.

Semi-automatic bus washers came into use at this time and the early ones had to be set to suit a 7ft 6in or 8ft-wide vehicle. To help garage staff identify the width of buses waiting to be washed, Salford fitted a red dome, similar in shape and size to a signalling bell, between the front upper-deck windows whilst Manchester's 8ft-wide buses had a red roof, the 7ft 6in ones remaining grey.

Manchester's 'thousands' fleet numbering scheme continued a practice started with the prewar trolleybuses, each new batch of buses commencing at the next 'round' number, such as 2110 or 3411. Thus there were, for example, no vehicles numbered 19, 26-29, 1238/9, 2109, 3403-3410, 4190-4199, 3793-3800 and 4685-4700. The numbers that were omitted varied over the years — largely according to the staff in charge at the time. These omissions could confuse the uninitiated and there was a celebrated letter to *The Manchester Evening News*

◄ Sir E. Leader Williams' 1890 iron aqueduct carrying the Bridgewater Canal over Barton Lane, Patricroft was to claim the upper half of several double-deckers in later years when drivers on the diverted Manchester/North Western 22 and LUT 87 had a lapse of memory. One of Salford's 10 Burlingham-bodied CVG6 single-deckers, 442, passes under the aqueduct on Salford service 5. The CVG6 was not normally offered in single-deck form but Daimler had built batches for Huddersfield and was prepared to build 15 more to allow Salford to use the same engine as in its double-deckers. *N. R. Knight*

The first of the second batch of Salford's Metro-Cammell bodied Daimler CVG6s, fleet numbers 456-560, photographed before delivery. The bodies differed slightly from the first batch in having polished aluminium frames for their opening windows. The Salford Taxation Office issued their FRJ registration numbers in April 1951, 15 months before the FRJ mark was generally issued, as Charles Baroth wanted all his buses to have "RJ" registrations. *Transport Vehicles (Daimler) Ltd*

appealing for details of 2109, for which the writer had searched for some years. The Department kindly sent him (or her) a copy of its fleet list.

AEC acquired Crossley Motors in 1948 and its first task was to design a new cylinder-head to replace the Crossley-designed unit that was the root cause of the DD42's engine problems. It worked but was expensive and both cities decided to run their Crossleys 'as is'. To help alleviate the problem in Manchester a considerable re-allocation of buses to garages took place in 1951. Queens Road became almost all Leyland, taking most of the PD1s and all the PD2s plus operation of the 98 service with its steep climb to Oldham and Waterhead. The Crossleys went to the more level services from Hyde Road and Birchfields Road garages, the interior rebuilding of the latter having just been completed. Parrs Wood became principally Leyland, Princess Road was a Daimler garage with the 4100-class and all the COG5s together with about half the CVG5s plus some Crossleys, whilst Northenden had all three makes — Daimlers, Crossleys plus Leyland TDs and PD1s.

By late 1948 the bodywork supply situation was easing and Manchester's final trams were abandoned in January 1949 with the delivery of Crossleys 2144-2151. This was done with due ceremony, although the tramcars were made to earn their last day's keep by working the morning rush hour — planned weeks ahead, this was not, as has oft been claimed, some sort of emergency measure. Many notable guests were invited to the ceremony and civic lunch at the Town Hall, including the Salford General Manager and the Chairman of the West Midlands Traffic Commissioners — R. Stuart Pilcher, CBE had come to see the fulfilment of his vision of 1929. Some have since said that Stuart Pilcher was blind to the merits of anything except the motorbus; in fact he had the vision of seeing what was best for the time. There seems little doubt that had he been in charge 25 years later, Manchester's new tramways would have been pressed forward with his unique and immense determination and might well have arrived all the sooner.

In 1949 Crossley began to build the trolleybuses for the long-delayed conversion of the Hyde service, which commenced on 15 January 1950 and was numbered 210, well away from the bus services. The reason for this apparently odd choice was that it was possible to fit '21' into the 'tens' track of a two-track Manchester number blind and the other trolleybus services were renumbered 211-219 in due course. Like the Stalybridge services the 210 was joint with SHMD but the latter had no trolleybuses and worked off its share of the mileage on bus service 125 to Glossop.

Metro-Cammell started on Salford's Daimler chassis in 1949 and the first entered service the following year, delivery being completed in 1952. They were magnificent vehicles, beautifully detailed and superbly finished. Later ones had green painted mudguards with the nearside front one squared-off back to the body. The single-decker order was subject to some change. Salford had three single-deck services, neatly numbered 4, 5 and 6. The 4 ran from Prestwich through suburban avenues and then along the narrow lane (hence the single-decker) to the tiny hamlet of Simister; until March 1946 it had been worked by small independent Parry of Simister.

The reason for single-deckers on the 5 (Peel Green) service was the low-clearance aqueduct carrying the Bridgewater Canal over Barton Lane, Patricroft. The road was also used by LUT and the long-established Manchester/North Western 22 (Levenshulme-Chorlton-Eccles) service in which Salford, incidentally, had no share. The aqueduct was to claim many double-deck victims in the years to come, particularly when the 22 was converted to double-deckers and drivers forgot the revised route. LUT crews did the same and that the 1890 iron aqueduct never leaked as a result of these collisions is a tribute to its designer, Ship Canal Engineer, Sir E. Leader Williams.

Service 6 (Eccles-Pendlebury-Prestwich-Radcliffe) had no low bridges but in Prestwich it did have the steep and (at that time) narrow and twisty Rainsough Brow which was considered dangerous for double-deckers. After careful tests, the Traffic Commissioners agreed to its operation with 7ft 6in-wide double-deckers and Burlingham's order for 15 single-deckers was revised to 10 single-deck buses (441-450), one committee coach (451) and four 7ft 6in-wide double-deckers (452-455) specifically for service 6. Burlingham's design was adapted to conform to the Salford specification, they were also Burlingham's first metal-framed bodies.

The last six Metro-Cammell Daimlers, 555-560, were fitted with saloon heaters for use on the all-night services and were rarely seen during the day. Manchester and Salford had a comprehensive network of all-night services, running approximately hourly, the two cities together having the best pre-PTE night bus network outside London. The all-night services were almost a separate operation, staffed by permanent night shift crews who never worked days and, in Salford's case, using dedicated vehicles.

The Manchester Leyland Tigers bought in 1930 for the express services were rebodied to the original design by the Car Works in the late 1930s. Several were converted to mobile staff canteens during and after the war and in this guise survived into the 1950s and 1960s. In a joint project with the PTE, fleetnumber 28 was rescued from a Bradford scrapyard, carefully restored to working condition and is now in the Museum of Transport.
Dennis Talbot

In 1939 the Car Works Apprentice School made this model of Crossley Mancunian 989, the first of the updated Streamliners which had a range of improvements including double-skin upper-deck roofs and higher-backed seats. It was on display in the window of the Department's enquiry and lost property office at 55 Piccadilly for many years (later being 'updated' as fleet number 2960). Restored to its original condition, it is now in the Museum of Transport.
R. L. Wilson

In fine condition for a 22 year-old bus, Leyland-bodied Leyland Titan TD5 Streamliner 3864 on 8 July 1961 at MCT's Chorlton Office. The bus was withdrawn in November of that year. The TD5s were fitted with a special-to-Manchester close-ratio gearbox which gave them a somewhat deeper sound compared with the standard model. The single-decker in the background on service 22 to Eccles is a particularly rare vehicle — one of North Western's two Willowbrook-bodied lightweight Atkinsons, fleetnumbers 512 and 513.
John Ryan

Stamford Street, Ashton-under-Lyne in 1955 with Manchester's English Electric-bodied Leyland TB5 trolleybus 1108, new in 1940, en route for Stevenson Square via Ashton New Road. 1108 has come straight down Stamford Street from Stalybridge; trolleybuses on short workings and service 219 which terminated in Ashton's Market Place would join using the overhead which comes in from the left of the picture. The Ashton New Road services from Stevenson Square were Manchester-operated, Ashton working its mileage share on the Ashton Old Road services from Piccadilly.
Photobus — J. Copland

On a sunny summer's day in 1955, Crossley Streamliner trolleybus 1155 passes the glass-fronted Daily Express building in Great Ancoats Street, outbound from Corporation Street to Greenheys on the 213 service. Behind is an English Electric-bodied Leyland Streamliner trolleybus and in the far background a Crossley crosses into Oldham Road. *Photobus — J. Copland*

Having survived into SELNEC as a dual-control training bus, 1940 Salford Park Royal-bodied AEC Regent 235 was acquired by Roy Marshall and placed on permanent loan to the Museum of Transport. It was then arranged that, if society members stripped it down to bare metal (the job took 60 gallons of paint remover), the Frederick Road paint shop would restore its exterior finish to 'as new'. By then spending their time applying 'boring masses of orange paint', the Salford team did the job with great enthusiasm, showing that it had lost none of its skills or pride in the job. Retired paintshop staff were brought in to advise, every square inch was rubbed down with steel wool and extra coats of varnish were applied 'to get the shade of red just right'.
The SELNEC painting schedule slipped by two weeks but the paintshop team recovered it and this was the splendid result. There were a great many 'oohs' and 'aahs' when 235 emerged through Frederick Road's archway in bright sunshine. *Roy Marshall*

Metro-Cammell/Crossley-bodied Leyland Titan TD5 3949 in Princess Street, bound for the picturesquely-named Fog Lane. Although the bus was 21 years old, its paintwork was smart and glossy and the TD5 would acquit itself well against the two new Daimler CVG6s following behind. The practice of painting the lower section of the radiator cowl black was quite common in the postwar years. 3949 was withdrawn in October 1961 shortly after this picture was taken. *Peter Roberts*

The rear of the Streamliner, showing the unusual divided rear lower-deck window. Leyland-bodied TD5 3934 on Oxford Road, All Saints on 24 June 1961. In the distance, outward bound and in original livery, is a Crossley-bodied Daimler CVG5 from the 4000-4049 batch. *John Ryan*

◄ Manchester's Metro-Cammell/Crossley-bodied Daimler COG5 4255 in Albert Square in 1960, about to return to Princess Road garage after the morning peak. New in 1940, the bus served the city for 21 years, being withdrawn in September 1961. In postwar years it was common practice to paint the radiator shells of older buses and some of the glamour of the COG's chrome-plated radiator shell was lost. Unlike many contemporary body designs, the curved profile of the Streamliner's body nicely matched the slope of the Daimler radiator.
Peter Roberts

▲ Manchester's last Crossley Mancunian, 2782, withdrawn in Hyde Road yard along with Daimler COG5s 4257 and 4265 and two Leyland Titan TD5s during an enthusiasts' visit on a cold winter's day in 1962. The last Manchester Crossley Mancunian to run in service was 2997, withdrawn in May 1957, but 2782 served as the mobile staff canteen in Piccadilly until the rebuilding of the bus station was completed in December 1958. It then remained in the yard until sold for scrap in 1963 along with the last Leyland TD5, 3917 and the last Daimler COG5, 4266. Plans were made to preserve all three and the Department was co-operative, asking only £62 for 3917, but bus preservation was in its infancy, there was nowhere to keep them and the attempt came to nought.
Peter Roberts

Manchester's Crossleys 'owed' from the pre-war orders arrived in 1946/7 and were numbered 2890-2959/61, well away from the 8ft-wide ones, which started at 2000. This is 2929, along with 7ft 6in PD1 3034 and an 8ft-wide Crossley, working a Maine Road football special on a warm day in the early 1950s. It may not, however, be a Manchester City home game because, after the Old Trafford ground was bombed during the war, Manchester United shared the Maine Road ground with their rivals for several years. *Peter Roberts*

Manchester Metro-Cammell-bodied Leyland PD1 3028 in Piccadilly on the 64 service to Ringway Airport on 6 October 1962. The grey roof signifies that the bus is 7ft 6in wide, enabling the garage staff to set the early automatic bus washers. Later machines did not need to be specially set and the grey roof was given up when the 'all-red' livery was introduced in 1957. Due to narrow roads in Sharston and Gatley, for many years it was a licence condition that the 64 be operated by 7ft 6in-wide buses. Excellent vehicles, when the last of the batch was withdrawn in 1966 it was as solid and rattle-free as the day it was delivered 19 years before. *Photobus — Roy Marshall*

▲ Compared with the PD1s and the Crossleys, Salford's 15 AEC Regent IIIs somehow looked more 'classy'. 273 has arrived early, having given its passengers a brisk run from Sandy Lane, Prestwich, and is waiting to pull onto the stand for service 40. In the left background are Crossley 252 and a fully loaded CVD6 on service 8 to Bolton. *Peter Roberts*

► Salford 1947 Leyland-bodied PD1 309 photographed near Pendleton Church working service 50 to Duchy Road. The framework, which carried the extended destination indicator handles down to a level at which crews could reach them from ground level, was a feature of Salford's postwar front-engined buses. *R. L. Wilson*

▲ A day at the races. Manchester Racecourse was in Salford and served by Salford buses. Salford Leyland PD1A 322 has a Leyland body whilst that on PD1 285 is by Metro-Cammell. The Leyland-bodied bus is one of 30 (313-342) which were offered by Leyland in 1948 because of a cancelled export order. Ordered as PD2s by their original purchaser, Salford had Leyland fit them with the smaller 7.4-litre engine. *Peter Roberts*

▶ Salford 343-350 were originally ordered by Chester Corporation. By the time they were being built in 1948 they were surplus to Chester's needs and Charles Baroth quickly arranged to take over the contract. Unlike the other Salford Daimlers, they had Daimler engines. After withdrawal by Salford in 1963, 348 passed to local contracting firm Roy & Partners and is seen here in Piccadilly. *Peter Roberts*

Forlorn and withdrawn, 1947 Brush-bodied Daimler CVG5 4056 in Hyde Road yard in 1969. So precise was Manchester's specification that it was difficult to find any external difference between the postwar standard bodies built by Metro-Cammell, Crossley and Brush. The clue is in the shape of the drip moulding above the rearmost windows where it passes onto the rear dome. The bus on the left is a Metro-Cammell, the moulding following the window line for a short distance; the Brush moulding continued beyond the window before dipping downwards and on the Crossley body the moulding continued in a straight line.
R. L. Wilson

Evening peak hour is approaching on 16 July 1965 with 1948 Crossley DD42/4 2047 coming in to the city from Hyde Road Garage for a short working on the 210. Outbound on Downing Street, working service 109 is 1949 Crossley DD42/8S 2155, one of eight (2152-2159) fitted with platform doors. 2047 was withdrawn in February 1966 and 2155 a year later.
John Ryan

When the government allowed the width of buses to be increased to 8ft from 7ft 6in, Manchester immediately altered all its orders to be so, going to the extent of accepting a delay in delivery. An improvement which it did not adopt quite so quickly was the larger Leyland 9.8-litre O.600-engined PD2, for the Department believed that the PD1 model with its smaller 7.4-litre engine working hard would give better economy. 3050-3099 and 3100-3199 were 8ft-wide and this picture taken in about 1955 shows 3175 on a football special near Manchester City's ground, with one of 3050-3099 behind it. 3175 is in its original livery and still has semaphore trafficators.
Peter Roberts

Manchester's three batches of 8ft-wide Crossley DD42s (2000-2108, 2110-2159 and 2160-2219), delivered from 1947 to 1949, differed externally only in small details such as front mudguards. This picture shows 2123 waiting for football crowds at Manchester City's Maine Road ground with another from the same batch behind. The bus is in its original livery, although its original extended front wings have been cut back to avoid damage and improve brake cooling.
Peter Roberts

The end of a very long line of Crossley motorbuses for Manchester which started with VM 3675 pictured earlier in this book. 2219 entered service in October 1949, but it was not Manchester's last new Crossley — the 1200- and 1240-class trolleybuses followed in 1950 and 1951. The bus was photographed in Market Street on 7 July 1962. The deeper nearside canopy housed the saloon heater unit with which 2214-2219 were equipped. *John Ryan*

Crossley 'Empire' trolleybus 1200 in Hyde Road, Gorton on 10 February 1962 outbound on the 210 service to Hyde. Behind is Salford Daimler CVG6 436 going to Reddish on the 77. The 210 was joint with SHMD which never owned trolleybuses and balanced its share of the 210 mileage by extra turns on joint motorbus services 6 and 125 to Glossop. *John Ryan*

Manchester's six-wheel Crossley Dominion trolleybus 1240 passes Ashton-under-Lyne Corporation Bond-bodied BUT four-wheeler fleetnumber 83 at the Piccadilly terminus in Portland Street. New in March 1951, the bus was photographed on 3 May 1963, eight weeks before it was withdrawn. The 16 Dominions were the only examples of the type and spent their lives at Hyde Road garage, normally only appearing at rush-hours on short workings on the Hyde Road and Ashton Old Road services. All were sold in 1963, 1250 survived into preservation and at the time of writing was in the Museum of Transport.
John Ryan

Salford 351, the first of 195 Metro-Cammell-bodied Daimler CVG6s delivered in 1950-1952, turning into Piccadilly Bus Station en route from Reddish to Pendlebury on the joint 57/77 service. Although it has been repainted without black wings and a silver roof, the bus still has the small red dome at the front of the upper-deck indicating that it is 8ft wide. *R. L. Wilson*

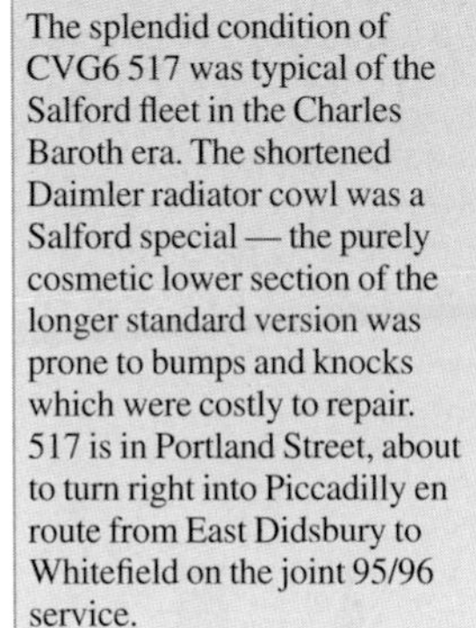
The splendid condition of CVG6 517 was typical of the Salford fleet in the Charles Baroth era. The shortened Daimler radiator cowl was a Salford special — the purely cosmetic lower section of the longer standard version was prone to bumps and knocks which were costly to repair. 517 is in Portland Street, about to turn right into Piccadilly en route from East Didsbury to Whitefield on the joint 95/96 service.
Photobus — Alastair Douglas

Tall and gaunt-looking because of their 7ft 6in width and with a tendency to lean on corners were Salford Burlingham-bodied CVG6s 452-455. This picture shows 454 at Weaste. They were ordered as single-deckers but the body contract was changed to double-deckers upon removal of the single-deck restriction at Rainsough Brow, Prestwich, on service 6. The bodies were the first that Burlingham built with steel frames.
Glen Bubb collection

The second Salford committee coach was this Burlingham-bodied Daimler CVG6. Seating only 22 it was equipped with every conceivable luxury, including wheel trims, tables, a sliding roof and radio. It had covered fewer than 10,000 miles when sold in 1962 to a Bury dealer; 451 then passed to Cheek's Coaches of Kenton, Middlesex where it ran for four years. This picture shows it on one of its rare excursions — in this case to Southport in 1957. Interestingly it did not carry the corporation's coat of arms. *Glen Bubb collection*

Now nicely restored and in the Museum of Transport, 1951 Metro-Cammell-bodied Leyland PD2/3 3245 was one of the last delivered with Manchester's standard postwar body which still retained vestiges of the prewar Streamliner. Excellent buses. *David Bielby*

Almost at the end of its life, with worn paintwork and the 'via' blind dropping out of its rollers, Queens Road has had to turn out 20 year-old Leyland PD2/3 3267 to replace a failed bus. 3267 is at the Chorlton terminus of cross-city service 82 to Waterhead, beyond Oldham. The route was 15 miles long with a climb of some 700ft, 3267 might be old but without doubt would have completed the day's work reliably. The Farington variant of the Leyland body with flush-fitting windows was relatively unusual — Manchester preferred flush-fitting windows because they made the bodywork easier to keep clean. *Peter Roberts*

If one had to choose candidates for postwar Glory Days buses in Manchester and Salford then top of the list would be Leylands 3200-3264, the 4100-class Daimlers and their Salford CVG6 counterparts. This is 4139 on a quiet 1958 afternoon in Piccadilly. New in 1951 the bus has had its first repaint, retaining the dark brown line separating cream from red (except at roof level, where it was never applied) which seemed to 'finish off' the livery. *Peter Roberts*

For many years Leyland-bodied PD2/12s 3330-3369, new in 1953, were Manchester's contribution to the joint 57/77 service. This is 3351 on 22 September 1962 in Deansgate en route to Reddish on service 77. The bus would shortly be called into the Car Works for a major overhaul during which it would be repainted into the 'all red' livery. *John Ryan*

Perhaps the most unusual of Manchester's post-war double-deckers and certainly the least photographed, were the 30 Northern Counties-bodied Leyland PD2/12s, 3300-3329. The thick central upper-deck window pillar contained the ducting for the Northern Counties 'air conditioning' system by which the air for the engine intake was ducted from the upper saloon. The bus is 3321, leaving Piccadilly on the then limited stop service 50 to Brooklands. On the left is Burlingham-bodied Daimler 4562 and North Western's East Lancs-bodied Dennis Loline 821 is on the right. *Peter Roberts*

◄ The final variation of the Salford livery was the elimination of two of the three primrose bands. This is one of the last of the CVG6s to be delivered, 548, about to turn into Victoria Bus Station having worked in from Lancaster Road on the 25/30 service. Several Salford services were pairs of circulars and the 30 went outwards via Bolton Road, returning via Weaste, the 25 working in the opposite direction. Services 27/28 and 70/71 were other circulars as were parts of the routes of the 19/21, 44/54, 64/66 and 57/77.
Photobus — Arnold Richardson

▼ Two of the 100 Leyland PD2/40s (3521-3620) delivered in 1958/9 had Cave-Browne-Cave heating systems. Developed by the professor of that name at Southampton University, the engine cooling radiators were either side of the front indicators. This is 3581, the first of the two, when new at the Barlow Moor Road terminus of service 41 in late 1959. *D. M. Eyre*

A Manchester bus in Yorkshire. Having travelled outwards via Lees as service 14, 1959 Leyland PD2/40 3604 has left Uppermill to return via Scouthead on service 13. Operated jointly with North Western and Oldham Corporation, the 13/14 worked as a circular through between Oldham and Uppermill. Although the bus would climb the western edge of the Pennines and travel through Oldham to reach the city some 15 miles away, 'Stevenson Square' was considered to be a sufficiently clear destination. *Photobus — P. Eckersley*

Manchester's 10 Park Royal-bodied Tiger Cubs delivered in 1961, 51-60, were finished in airport livery and known as the 'blue singles', the last six being dual-door. All ten had coach seats and luggage boots in order that they could be used to supplement the raised-roof airport coaches on the busy airport service. At other times they worked feeder and peak-hour express services and this picture shows fleetnumber 55 in 1966 at the Benchill Hotel terminus of Wythenshawe local service 148 to Peel Hall and Wythenshawe Civic Centre. The driver drinks a cup of tea supplied by the lady in the picture, who featured in *The Manchester Evening News* after she discovered that there were no tea-making facilities at either terminus of the 148 and generously took it upon herself to provide a brew. *Peter Roberts*

◀ The George Street section of Piccadilly Bus Station in the snow, with a Metro-Cammell-bodied PD1 from Northenden garage and one of Birchfields Road's Metro-Cammell Orion-bodied Leyland PD2s. In the background are the towers of the Piccadilly Plaza buildings. *Peter Roberts*

◀ When built Princess Parkway was an attractive road, lined with parkland, trees, cycleways and footpaths. All were obliterated in the construction of the M56 motorway. A Tiger Cub airport coach makes its way round the Wythenshawe Road roundabout, with a 'blue single' Tiger Cub and a Daimler Fleetline in the background. *Peter Roberts*

The Manchester Evening News called them 'Red Dragons'; delivered at the end of 1959 they spent several months in store whilst an agreement for their use was negotiated with the trade union. This is one of Manchester's first 10 Leyland Atlanteans, 3628, on 20 May 1961 at Parrs Wood working the 40 service. The last two of the batch, 3629/30, had air suspension. *John Ryan*

In 1961 several Salford Daimlers were painted in reversed livery to mark Salford Civic Week. This is 469, outbound on service 30 in Bolton Road, Pendleton. The livery is similar to that applied to four buses of the same type in 1953 to mark the Coronation. *R. L. Wilson*

Not quite what it seems, for the green buses behind Daimler Fleetline 4606 belong not to Salford but to Liverpool Corporation. Photographed at the famous Pier Head terminus on 20 February 1963, Liverpool borrowed 4606, one of Manchester's first batch of 20 Fleetlines, for evaluation purposes. The visit was to no avail — Liverpool bought Atlanteans. *John Ryan*

After the cancellation of the order in 1929 it was somehow unlikely that Manchester would ever buy AECs but it did have demonstrators on loan from time to time. Most notable were the two London buses. First was RT19, which gave Wilmslow Road customers a few brisk rides on the 41 in 1941 — the Department took some of the vehicle's design ideas into the post-war Crossleys. In February 1963 the RT's successor, the Routemaster, arrived on loan in the shape of RM1414 and it too impressed passengers and crews alike on the 41, 42, 161 and 162 services. Much later, London Transport generously donated the body and chassis units then carrying fleet number RM1414 to the Museum of Transport but this picture is of the genuine article in February 1963 at Barlow Moor Road, Southern Cemetery. *Neville Knight*

◄ A Manchester bus in London. New in 1963, Metro-Cammell Orion-bodied Daimler CVG6 4632 passed to SELNEC and GMT and when withdrawn was bought by Dennis Talbot, Chairman of the Museum of Transport, where it is now part of the collection. This picture was taken on 12 August 1985 at the end of a Chiswick Works Open Day. Still powered by its original Gardner 6LW engine, 4632 covered the 400-mile journey as easily as a day on service 92. *Dennis Talbot*

▲ A wet cold 1963 day with Salford's first Leyland PD2 at the Weaste terminus of service 3, its windows streaming with condensation. A non-trivial problem in the damp North West, condensation made the journey uncomfortable for passengers, made the bus grubby and unattractive and also caused corrosion. To combat it both cities began to fit heaters to their buses and Manchester experimented with forced-ventilation controlled-temperature systems on Fleetline 4628 and Atlantean 3723. *R. L. Wilson*

The all-conquering PD2 eventually arrived very late in Salford. Fleetnumbers 151-188 were delivered in 1963 in the single cream stripe livery. The Victoria Bus Station duty inspectors kept a close eye on the photographer and the conductor of 163 seems not to have been too impressed. Above is the Exchange Station approach and the station wall itself can just be seen. *Peter Roberts*

With the tower of Manchester Cathedral in the background, Daimler Fleetline 4655 turns from Victoria Street into Cateaton Street en route from Whitefield to East Didsbury on the Manchester/Salford joint 95/96 service. The 95 went via Great Clowes Street (the route devised by Salford at the start of the century to get its trams to Prestwich without crossing into Manchester) whereas the 96 went direct along Bury New Road. The service was every eight minutes, alternately a 95 and a 96, and if the bus at the front of the rush-hour queue at Whitefield was a 95 it would leave empty as regular passengers knew that the following 96 would arrive in town first. *R. L. Wilson*

The Metro-Cammell Orion bodies on Manchester PD2s from fleetnumber 3521 had a special-to-Manchester upright front profile, which allowed more room in the upper-deck. The city's 35 contemporary Daimler CVG6s did not have this feature — it was not worth the additional re-design cost for so few buses. Leylands from 3300 also had the optional chrome-plated pressed steel radiator cowl, which cost less to repair than the cast aluminium unit. Brand new 3651 in Cannon Street in October 1962. The bus also has its rear wheel trims in place — a great source of annoyance to tyre fitters and the cause of overheated brakes, they were discarded at any convenient opportunity, the usual excuse on the Bus Condition Report Form being 'fell off in service'.
Photobus — Roy Marshall

In the financial year 1963/4 both Manchester (fleetnumbers 4650-4654) and Salford (189, 190) were persuaded to try Daimler's CCG6 chassis, which had a Guy constant-mesh gearbox. Offered at low price they were not a bargain, drivers in both cities found the combination of Guy gearbox and Daimler chassis difficult to handle, although the box worked well enough in the Guy chassis. This is Salford 190 on service 2 at Manchester Docks in July 1967. Note the wider version of the 'Manchester' radiator cowl, necessitated by the wider-spaced chassis frame.
Photobus — Roy Marshall

Traffic requirements permitting, the first duty of a newly delivered Manchester bus was a short rush-hour journey, the intent being that any minor problems could be discovered and quickly attended to when the bus returned to garage. This is Hyde Road's new Leyland PD2/37 3674 on its first trip in March 1963. There were very few journeys on service 86/86X (Whalley Range-Clayton Bridge) which was an odd remnant of the former Chorlton-Glossop express service 6. Unlike most of the other express services, which were split in the early 1930s in the city centre at the behest of the Chief Constable, the 6 was only divided at the outbreak of the war in order to save fuel. Short workings 6A and 6B (renumbered 6X and later 86/86X) were not split and continued into SELNEC. *Photobus — Roy Marshall*

Salford Atlantean 211, new in 1964, in Piccadilly Bus Station is passed by 1963 Manchester Daimler Fleetline 4625. Both buses have Metro-Cammell bodies, the Salford one having the Manchester-designed front end with wrap-around windscreen introduced in that year on 4655, having been prototyped on 4628. *Peter Roberts*

A wet Sunday afternoon in Agecroft. With the power station and its cooling towers in the background, 1966 Leyland PD2 253 is on one of the unusual Salford services — the 34 ran every half-hour on Sunday afternoons from Pendleton to the Langley Road entrance of Agecroft Cemetery. Correctly titled 'Northern Cemetery' it was the geographical counterpart of the better known Southern Cemetery.
Photobus — P. Eckersley

In the early 1960s Manchester's view of the future was that one-man-operated high capacity single-deckers would become the norm. Its opinions were influential in the industry and at Manchester's instigation, Leyland introduced the Panther Cub and Manchester ordered 20 'off the drawing board'. Park Royal bodied them, the design featuring a double-width front-entrance and a narrow centre-exit. With the approval of one-person operation of double-deckers in 1966, Manchester immediately changed tack and led the industry to purpose-designed, one-man double-deckers. Panther Cub 63 turns from Piccadilly into Portland Street on the City Circle. Fleetnumber 74 is preserved in the Museum of Transport.
Peter Roberts

Manchester Atlantean 3770, new in 1965, descending Drake Street into Rochdale centre in July 1969 with an Oldham PD3 in the background. The Atlantean carries a slip board to indicate that it has a conductor and is not one-man operated. A board reading 'CONDUCTOR OPERATED' meant a two-man bus (and higher fare) whilst 'TEMPORARY CONDUCTOR' meant that there was no one-man bus available and a two-man bus was being used but that the fares were the lower, one-man rate. Fine in theory, the wording gave great scope for confusion by passengers and crews alike. It also created passenger hostility where two-man and one-man services ran along the same road — same journey, two different fares — and the two tier structure was soon replaced by a simpler Johnson Farebox-based system. *Photobus — Roy Marshall*

Seven-month-old Daimler Fleetlines 4702 and 4703 in Hyde Road garage on 12 June 1966. The Fleetlines and Atlanteans delivered in 1964, 1965, 1966 and 1967 had a Manchester-designed front added to the usual Metro-Cammell body. Initially a one-piece windscreen was used but it proved costly to replace if broken; the 38xx and 47xx batches had two-piece units and many of the earlier 4655-4684 batch were changed. The picture shows a curious variation, for 4703's front panel is of the type used on 4655-4684, which had a heater and demister air-intake grille — a different system was used on this batch but Metro-Cammell built 4703 with a front from the previous batch with the grille blanked off. The unpainted AEC on the right of the picture is Liverpool Corporation A40, the occasion being a visit by the Liverpool University Transport Society. *John Ryan*

Charles Baroth would certainly not have approved but needs must and in 1968 Salford's buses finally started to carry external advertising. Still in excellent condition, 15 year-old Daimler CVG6 543 is on Bolton Road inbound from Duchy Road to King Street, Manchester. Correctly, the bus shows 'Manchester' as its destination — the only place that a Salford bus displayed 'SALFORD' on its indicator was the hand-amended picture on the front of the Salford timetable.
Photobus — Roy Marshall

Bolton Town Hall provides an imposing background for this shot of new Salford Atlantean 290 at the then Howell Croft South terminus of service 8 to Salford in 1968. A joint Salford, Bolton and LUT service and the divided half of the former Hyde-Bolton express, the timetable (every 12/15 minutes) remained almost unchanged from 1930 and, with 38 minutes allowed for the 10-mile journey, required some spirited running once clear of the congested city and town areas.
Photobus — P. Eckersley

With a backdrop of Bolton and Rivington Moor, former 1967 Salford Metro-Cammell-bodied Leyland PD2 265, renumbered 3111 by SELNEC, makes its way along Smethurst Lane, Daubhill, Bolton. Service 12 took a roundabout route, leaving Bolton in almost the opposite direction to Salford and going via Daubhill, Little Hulton, Walkden, Roe Green and Worsley. The journey took 55 minutes as opposed to the 38 minutes of direct service 8. *Photobus — P. Eckersley*

Newly-delivered Salford Park Royal-bodied dual-door Atlantean 304 at the Peel Green terminus of the 64/66 service in September 1969. SELNEC was to add to the cross-city links by joining the 64/66 with the former trolleybus service 219 to Ashton-under-Lyne, the resulting services keeping their Salford numbers. The style of body was an interim design evolved by Park Royal and did not lend itself very happily to the Salford livery, which emphasised the shallowness of the front upper-deck windows.
Photobus — P. Eckersley

A sunny day at Manchester International Airport with Manchester's turquoise and white liveried Plaxton-bodied Bedford VAL fleetnumber 206 arriving on the express service from the city. The Department's plan to have a fleet of 12 coaches, replacing half of them each year with new vehicles, was overtaken by SELNEC's wider coaching ambitions.
R. L. Wilson

A big bus in a narrow road and a seemingly odd location for a city bus. The Manchester Panthers were renumbered by SELNEC and several then moved to Salford's garages, from which they worked single-deck services 4 and 5. This is SELNEC 52 (Manchester 97) making its way cautiously along Simister Lane on service 4 to the hamlet of Simister, near Prestwich. Simister became famous as the oft-congested Junction 18 of the M62 and M66, which is virtually on top of the tiny village. *Photobus — Arnold Richardson*

Daimler Fleetline Mancunian 2048 was displayed by Park Royal on its stand at the 1968 Commercial Motor Show along with more traditionally styled Sheffield Atlantean 293. When the show was over, the Department arranged for both buses to be put on display in Manchester on 26 October along with Newcastle Corporation 601, an Alexander-bodied Atlantean with an unusual nearside staircase, and the public were asked for their opinions on all three. In the following days the three buses worked on the 19 (Victoria Station-Reddish) service. Notice the British Leyland badge fitted above 2048's windscreen for the Show. *Peter Roberts*

▲
The second batches of Mancunians were 33ft long, and the extra capacity produced the first 100-passenger one-man double-decker. This is Atlantean 1051 when new at the terminus of the 53 service at Queens Road.
Photobus — Arnold Richardson

Daimler Fleetline Mancunian 2086 leaving Hyde Road garage. A cherished feature of Manchester's garages can be seen in this picture — the brass war memorial plaque, which recorded the names of staff members lost in the war. The plaques were carefully maintained and highly polished. ▶
Photobus — Arnold Richardson

◂ The sun shines on London Road, Manchester in July 1970. Looking towards Piccadilly, a Mancunian is outbound on the 94, going inwards are an Ashton Corporation Roe-bodied Leyland PD2, one of Manchester's Leyland-bodied Leyland PD2s from the 3330 batch, a Salford PD2 on the 95/96 service, a Manchester CVG6 and, almost hidden, a Fleetline.
Photobus — P. Eckersley

Park Royal-bodied Leyland Atlantean 1107 from the third order for Mancunians, outbound on Oxford Road. New to SELNEC in March 1970 the bus was one of the last to be delivered in full Manchester livery. Deliveries in April and onwards had the city coat of arms omitted and the next orders were finished in SELNEC sunglow orange livery.
The driving position on the first two batches of Mancunians was found to be rather low and was raised by some nine inches on the third and subsequent ones.
Photobus — Arnold Richardson

Bound for Leigh, 1965 Salford Atlantean 228 draws up to a Lancashire United bus stop at Worsley Station near the junction of Worsley Road and Greenleach Lane in May 1969. In days gone by, there would have been trolleybus overhead for the SLT service from Atherton to Farnworth via Swinton. A tiny remnant remained — the bus stop on the left-hand side still reads 'Trolleybuses Stop Here'.
Photobus — P. Eckersley

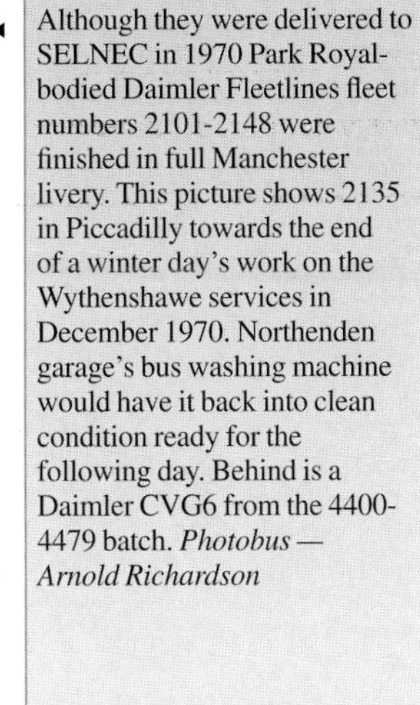

Although they were delivered to SELNEC in 1970 Park Royal-bodied Daimler Fleetlines fleet numbers 2101-2148 were finished in full Manchester livery. This picture shows 2135 in Piccadilly towards the end of a winter day's work on the Wythenshawe services in December 1970. Northenden garage's bus washing machine would have it back into clean condition ready for the following day. Behind is a Daimler CVG6 from the 4400-4479 batch. *Photobus — Arnold Richardson*

Manchester's East Lancashire-bodied Mancunians differed in many details from the Park Royal and Metro-Cammell build and did not 'gel'.
The pillar spacing was perhaps more pleasing but the misplacing of the boundary between red and white above the lower-deck windows spoiled them and, with other slightly odd details, resulted in a less neat appearance than the Park Royal and Metro-Cammell bodies. One result of this was that SELNEC specified very precisely the width and positioning of the orange and white bands of its new livery. Leyland Atlantean 1134 at Trafford Bar on 22 February 1971. *John Ryan*

▲
Salford's 20 Mancunians had Leyland Atlantean chassis and Metro-Cammell bodies, generally similar to Manchester's Fleetlines 2151-2210. Delivered new to SELNEC in 1970 and numbered 1201-1220, they had Salford interiors and indicators, and registration numbers (SRJ 324-343H) to match their intended Salford fleet numbers. This picture shows 1207 leaving Victoria Bus Station. *Photobus — Arnold Richardson*

New in service, SELNEC's 'Salford Mancunian' 1210 arriving from Walkden on 7 June 1970. The crew has already changed the destination indicator in readiness for the outward journey and upper-deck passengers are making their way to the staircase ready to alight as the bus pulls onto the service 9 stand in Victoria Bridge Street. 1210 is passing SELNEC PD2 3050 (formerly Salford 201) and is followed by a Park Royal-bodied Atlantean arriving from Peel Green. The drivers of both Atlanteans are wearing their light-coloured summer jackets. *John Dugdale* ►

▲
The contract for Manchester's last 34 Mancunians, fleet numbers 2271-2304, was won by East Lancs but when its works was virtually destroyed by fire in 1970 the firm asked to be released from the contract. Park Royal was busy and the contract was passed to group-member Roe, which did its usual high quality job. They were delivered to SELNEC finished in sunglow orange and this picture shows brand new 2299 on 26 April 1972 arriving in the again-rebuilt Chorlton Street Bus Station on express service 121 from Middleton and Langley. *John Ryan*

10. Glory Days in Manchester

In 1965, both general managers retired, Charles Baroth to a long and contented retirement. By contrast, and in somewhat similar manner to Stuart Pilcher, Albert Neal was sought out by the government to become Special Adviser to the then Minister of Transport, Mrs Barbara Castle, to advise on the structure and duties of the Passenger Transport Executives. How much the somewhat sudden approval of one-person operation of double-deckers in 1966 was also due to the influence of the Minister of Transport's newly appointed Special Adviser is a matter for conjecture.

Both new general managers came from other Lancashire municipalities. Salford's John Craggs came from Widnes. At Salford he had the support of several long-serving members of Charles Baroth's team and things continued much as before — even to the extent of Salford's continuing to resist external advertisements on its buses until a year before SELNEC took over. Manchester had succumbed, albeit reluctantly, in 1950. A Charles Baroth ruse to avoid this had been the resiting of the Salford coat of arms to the upper-deck side panels 'to reduce the cost of replacing damaged lower-deck panels'.

Manchester's new general manager was Ralph Bennett. Already highly respected in the industry and noted for innovation at his previous post, Bolton, he was a man cast very much in the mould of Stuart Pilcher. In a very short space of time Manchester's bus fleet and its operations would be transformed, although in saying this it is important to acknowledge that the foundations for what was about to happen had been laid in Albert Neal's last five years.

Bright new liveries, purpose-designed one-man double-deckers of strikingly modern appearance, luxury coaches for private hire, new methods of fare collection, innovative pricing policies, efficiency-seeking service revisions, new forms of timetable, and a more open, friendly image for the Department burst upon the Manchester scene. It was a return to the glory days of Stuart Pilcher.

In October 1965 the Panther Cubs, with their wide front entrances, were deployed on a group of services with the catchingly-named Minimax fare system — a 3d/6d (1.25, 2.5p) fare for any distance. Highly successful, it was eventually extended to double-deckers and the busy 53 service. As with the first tram conversion, one-man operation and the crush loaders, the test was that if it would work on the 53, then it would work anywhere.

On 1 July 1966 the Government approved driver-only operation of double-deckers and at its next meeting on 3 August 1966 the City Council agreed with Ralph Bennett's proposal to change completely to one-man bus operation with future vehicles being specifically designed for this purpose. Manchester was not the first to put a one-man double-decker in service because negotiating the necessary agreements with the unions for total changeover was a complex task that took exactly a year. What was important was that Manchester was the first large operator to commit to and press ahead with total conversion.

The change would, in time, be followed by the rest of the industry and a measure of the huge contribution that the Manchester team made to the bus industry may be judged by the fact that in 1965 one-person operation of double-deckers was illegal; barely three years later, when the Government introduced a scheme of grants for purchase of new buses, a qualifying double-decker had to be capable of one-person operation.

Not every innovation went according to plan, nor should it, for pioneering involves taking risks and the skill is to decide whether to persevere, modify or try an alternative. For example, experiments with fare systems included Autoslot machines, turnstiles, lower fares for one-man operated services compared with conductor operated ones. The latter caused some confusion when, because of vehicle shortages, a two-man operated bus had to be sent out to work a one-man service, or when two-man and one-man buses ran along the same roads. Eventually things settled down to a simplified fare structure using the American Johnson fare-box for fare collection. By mid-1969 some 60 of Manchester's 120 principal bus services were one-man operated with further conversions limited only by the rate of delivery of new buses.

In the mid- and late-1960s vehicle delivery times were lengthy, with orders needing to be placed up to three years in advance. On 13 October 1965 the City Council approved Ralph Bennett's proposal to order 48 Atlanteans and a similar number of Fleetlines with bodies by Park Royal, styled by the Department. The City Council also agreed to modify the livery, commencing

KEYDATES

1965 - Charles Baroth retires, John Craggs becomes SCT general manager
- Albert Neal retires, Ralph Bennett becomes MCT general manager
Oct - Minimax flat fares introduced by MCT
Nov - order placed for 96 Mancunian double-deckers with Park Royal bodies

1966 3 Aug - MCT decision to adopt one-man double-deckers
Dec - Bedford VAL/Plaxton coaches enter service with MCT - last MCT trolleybus

1967 May – MCT Autoslot ticket system for one-man double-deckers
Jul – MCT three-level fare structure
Sep – MCT first one-man double-deckers into service
Oct – MCT Autoslot and turnstile Panthers on 123
31 Dec – last MCT Crossley withdrawn (2152)
– SCT orders 20 Mancunians

continued

KEYDATES continued

1968 Feb – Mancunian 1001 handed over at Leyland. Public launch and display of Mancunian in Piccadilly
Apr – Mancunians enter service from Hyde Road on 19 and 169/170
– MCT adopts the Johnson farebox
– East Lancs-bodied Mancunians ordered, some with single door
– Ralph Bennett leaves MCT to become Chief Executive of London Transport
– Jack Thompson becomes MCT general manager
– SCT external advertising introduced

1969 Jan – 100-passenger double-decker,1051, enters service

with the 30 Panthers ordered the previous year, and to change the Department's title to Manchester City Transport — similar to that which Charles Baroth had selected for Salford in 1946.

During the rest of 1965 and 1966 Park Royal worked with the Department on the design of the new buses. As it evolved the decision to change to one-man operation was taken and the layout was altered to dual-door, with a wide front entrance (introduced on the Panther Cubs) which could accommodate two streams of passengers, each of which would pay their fares into an Autoslot ticket machine mounted by the bulkheads. To save time waiting for passengers to alight a similarly wide centre exit was introduced. Seats were provided for 45 upstairs and 28 in the lower-deck, the forward ones of which faced inwards to allow 23 standing passengers, giving a total vehicle capacity of 96, the floor being strengthened to carry this extra weight.

Industrial designers were asked to advise on the external design. 'A bus is a box', they said, 'and a box is an honest shape. Why disguise it with false peaks and domes?' The striking external appearance was achieved by accentuating the sharp corners and using crisp, clean outlines and large window sizes. The very large vertical windscreen, with curved corners, gave the driver an excellent view of the road and was visually striking, although it was costly to replace if broken and could cause awkward interior reflections in the driver's cab at night. All in all, the end result was as advanced and good-looking as Stuart Pilcher's Streamliners.

Whilst all this was going on, the final trolleybus conversion was completed with no civic ceremony at the end of December 1966. In May 1967 all but one of the Panthers arrived, finished in the new livery. Bus 100 was destroyed by fire at Metro-Cammell's works and was not replaced — Manchester's priorities had moved to one-man double-deckers and the Panthers and Panther Cubs would have only short lives in the city.

The Manchester Crossleys went (2152 was the last in December 1967) as did the immediate postwar CVG5s (4075 in September 1968) and the PD1s (3163/6 in October 1969); at Salford more CVG6s were replaced by 21 Metro-Cammell-bodied Atlanteans in 1968 and 20 with standard Park Royal bodies which arrived in 1969. The older vehicles' passing was marked by various enthusiasts' farewell tours but what everyone was waiting for were Ralph Bennett's new double-deckers. He decided that the new type of bus should have a name and the Department ran a competition, the result of which was awaited with some trepidation, having seen some of the entries.

Everyone was pleased when the Department announced the winner, which was 'Mancunian' — the name of a person born in the city, it was also the name of the Crossley chassis built to the Department's specification back in the 1930s.

More excitement was generated when it was announced that there would be a public launch with sample vehicles on display in Piccadilly. The fleet numbering was also changed — intended to be 3901-3948 and 4801-4848 (matching registration numbers were obtained), it was then decided that to allow for future deliveries they would be numbered 1001 up (Atlanteans) and 2001 up for the Fleetlines. As they neared completion at Park Royal's works, it became clear that the large area of cream paint looked yellowish against the smaller areas of vermilion and some were therefore finished in white instead of cream. Interestingly, as in the days of the Streamliners, the new livery was only applied to vehicles designed to carry it and the rest of the fleet continued in the previous scheme but with white instead of cream for the single band.

The first Mancunian to be finished was 1001 which was handed over to the Chairman of the Transport Committee by the Chairman of Leyland Motors, Sir Donald Stokes, at Leyland on 19 February 1968. On Saturday 24 February 1001 (red/white) and 1024 (red/cream) were put on display in Piccadilly and passengers and crews alike were given short free rides and asked to complete a questionnaire on colour (white or cream), entrance, staircase, seats, layout and general attractiveness. The event attracted so many people that it was repeated the following weekend. The livery vote went heavily to white and the five cream buses were soon repainted white.

These events became normal Manchester practice. After Fleetline 2048 had been proudly displayed by Park Royal at the 1968 Commercial Motor Show it was put on display in Piccadilly along with a new Sheffield Atlantean, which had also been at the show and a 1966-built one, converted to dual-door, from Newcastle-upon-Tyne. In this case the event was staged with some civic pride as if to say 'Look how advanced is the City of Manchester' — although both the other buses had novel features. When the new East Lancs-bodied Mancunians arrived in 1969, just before SELNEC took over, 1133 along with Fleetline 2090 was put on display in Piccadilly, signwritten 'THIS IS YOUR NEW BUS'.

Sufficient Mancunians had arrived by the end of March 1968 and on the first day of April they went into service from Hyde Road Garage on the busy 19 (Reddish via Gorton) and 169/170

(Droylsden-Belle Vue-West Didsbury) services, although 1004 was used on a few journeys on the 50 (East Didsbury) service from Parrs Wood garage the previous week in order to be sure that there would be no snags 'on the day'. Subsequently the Mancunians went to all the garages — Fleetlines and Atlanteans alike.

Even though it was clear that the PTE would take over in 1969, vehicle delivery times were lengthy and four more orders for Mancunians were placed, making a grand total of 472, the final order being won entirely by Daimler. Each batch incorporated experience from the previous ones — driving positions were modified, staircases were improved, experience with loading times and worries concerning accidents prompted 1131-1142 to be built with single entrances, and so on. Most were built by Park Royal but East Lancs had developed an excellent relationship with Ralph Bennett at Bolton and gained two orders for Mancunians — it built the 1131-1154 batch but the disastrous fire at its works in 1970 caused the firm to ask to be relieved of the second order (2271-2304), which was eventually passed to Roe. Metro-Cammell also got back some of Manchester's business and built 2151-2210. There were subtle differences between batches but, as in the previous glory days, essential parts were standardised.

◄ Metro Cammell was Manchester's preferred body supplier from 1932 to 1968 and was not happy when it lost the first Mancunian order to Park Royal. It won the second order but but then found its works overloaded and was forced to sub-contract the order to Park Royal. The fourth order for Mancunians was for 34 Leyland Atlanteans with Park Royal bodies and 60 Metro Cammell-bodied Daimler Fleetlines (2151-2210), all being delivered to Selnec in orange livery. The Metro Cammell bodies were readily identified by the removable panel between the headlights and the wider spacing of the fog lamps. This picture shows Northenden's 2198 in Piccadilly when new. *Photobus - Arnold Richardson*

KEYDATES

1969 1 Nov – SCT and MCT become part of SELNEC

1972 1 May – Last MCT-ordered vehicles, Mancunians 2274/5/8/82/87/92/4/5/7/8, 2300, enter service

1979 Mancunian 1001 restored by GMT to MCT livery and placed in Museum of Transport

11. Sunglow Sunset

Scarcely had the first Mancunian arrived than Ralph Bennett left to become Chief Executive of London Transport. It was perhaps the only job that could have attracted him away from Manchester, although it turned out to be something of a poisoned chalice beset by political interference. His successor was his well-liked and popular deputy, Jack Thompson.

On 1 November 1969, the SELNEC Passenger Transport Executive took over the Manchester and Salford undertakings, along with those of Stockport, Ashton-under-Lyne, SHMD, Oldham, Rochdale, Bury, Ramsbottom, Bolton and Leigh. Its formation was much disliked by several of the councils who were opposed to giving up their bus undertakings and losing control of services and fares; some saw the PTE as nothing more than Manchester finally achieving its long-held ambitions.

Some Mancunians were delivered to SELNEC in red livery; others came in SELNEC's sunglow orange — a list will be found elsewhere in this book. The final words, however, must go to John Craggs and Salford City Transport, for he it was who, perhaps, built the ultimate bridge between the two cities when he placed an order for 20 of Ralph Bennett's Atlantean Mancunians. Delivery times were such that they did not arrive until SELNEC and were therefore finished in sunglow orange and never carried their intended Salford fleet numbers, although they had Salford's indicator layout and their interior was pure Salford. One felt that by doing so John Craggs laid the foundation for SELNEC's integration and the re-creation of John Greenwood's integrated transport system.

SELNEC structured its initial operations into three divisions, Central, North and South, with Manchester and Salford forming the Central Division, managed largely but not entirely by former Manchester staff. Inevitably this led to unhappiness in Salford, which surfaced as a dispute in 1970 when SELNEC announced its fleet renumbering scheme, which was based on Manchester's system, likewise the proposed service renumbering. In fact the schemes were devised by Geoffrey Harding, Director of Operations and Engineering, who had never worked at Manchester, and Chief Engineer Harry Taylor, whose background was Liverpool and who had been general manager at Oldham.

Nevertheless, Salford councillors objected to the renumbering of their buses into the Manchester series and to altering all the Salford service numbers. A compromise was negotiated — all the Salford buses would be renumbered, using Manchester fleetnumber transfers, but its service numbers would not be changed. To balance this, Manchester's single-deck buses would also be renumbered (a totally pointless exercise) and its service numbers would be changed where they clashed with those of Salford. The formal justification for the latter was that Salford's buses only had two-track number blinds, the fact that something like 1,000 Manchester vehicles were the same being conveniently ignored. Of such compromises are bridges built and it was not long before Manchester single-deckers were running from Weaste and Frederick Road, and Salford double-deckers operating from Manchester garages.

In 1974, with local government reorganisation, SELNEC became the Greater Manchester Passenger Transport Executive, colloquially 'GMT', and its culture increasingly became that of a large corporation transport department serving the whole conurbation. Maybe the Manchester City Council of 1895 was right after all.

Further reading

The Manchester Carriage & Tramways Company — Ted Gray — (no ISBN)

The Manchester Tramways — Ian Yearsley and Philip Groves — ISBN 086317 144 3

Salford's Tramways Part 1 and Part 2 — Ted Gray — ISBN 187011 947 9

The Manchester Bus — Michael Eyre and Chris Heaps — ISBN 086317 151 6

Salford City Transport — Ted Gray — ISBN 090383 906 7

Fleet History PC7 — SELNEC — The PSV Circle

Fleet History PC10 — Salford — The PSV Circle

THE FLEETS

The detail in these lists is summarised, more complete details can be found in the references in "Further reading"

A explanation of ABBREVIATIONS used in the list appears on page 111

MANCHESTER CARRIAGE AND TRAMWAYS COMPANY LTD

Horsetram and horsebus fleet at 31 March 1901

	Single-deck Double-ended	Double-deck Reversible	Double-deck Double-ended	Double-deck Double-ended Workmen's	Double-deck Reversible Workmen's	Single-deck Reversible	Horse Bus
DIVISION							
Cheetham Hill	C.2-3	C.4-6, 9-36	C.7-8	–	–	–	–
Harpurhey	–	HY.4, 9-33	HY.5-8	HY.35,40	HY.36-39	–	–
Oldham & Openshaw	–	O.1-3/5-24, 26-35/7-44/6/7/9/50, 94-100	–	O25, 45,48	–	O.51-4/6-60, 62-93	–
Longsight	–	L.1-3/5-9, 12-39, 41-78, 80-107/10-26/8/9/33-45	– –	L.130-2	–	L.11, 40, 108/9	L.1-23
Hulme	H.77/8	H.1-48/50-8, 76/9-87/9-97	–	–	–	H.59-64/6-75, 98	–
Broughton	–	B.1-17	–	–	–	B.21-34/6/8	–
Pendleton	–	P.1-29, 31/3-9,42	–	–	–	–	–
Weaste	–	W.1-37	–	–	–	–	–

Bought by Manchester: trams C.24-9/31/2/4-6, horse buses L1-23;

Bought by Salford: trams B.15-17/21-34/6/8; P.1-29, 31/3-9, 42; W.1-37

CITY OF SALFORD

Tramcars

Year	Fleet nos	Type	Builder	Body	Withdrawn	Note
1901	1-100	4-wheel	Milnes	Open top double-deck	1936-9	A
1902-3	101-130	Bogie	Milnes	Open top double-deck	1939-47	B
1903	131-150	Bogie	BEC	Open top double-deck	1939-47	C
1905	151-160	Bogie	UEC	Single-deck, part open sides, part closed	1912	D
1905	161-162	Bogie	BEC	Open top double-deck	1907,1947	E
1905	163-172	4-wheel	UEC	Double deck, open platform	1936-7	F
1905	173-177	4-wheel	BEC	Double-deck open top, open platform	1935-8	G,H
1907-8	177-196	4-wheel	UEC	Double deck, open platform	1935-9	
1907-8	197-200	4-wheel	Hurst Nelson	Double deck, open platform	1935-9	
1913-4	151-160	4-wheel	Brush	Double deck, open top, enclosed platform	1939-47	J
1914-5	201-212	Bogie	Brush	Double deck, enclosed platform	1946-7	
1915	213-224	Bogie	Brush	Double deck, open top, enclosed platform	1939-47	L
1923-5	225-230	4-wheel	Brush	Double deck, fully enclosed	1946-7	K

A *1905 onwards some fitted with top covers, some later fitted with enclosed platforms. In 1926 1-93/5-100 were renumbered 231-329 to bring the top-covered cars together. From 1926*

B *All fitted with top-covers by 1924, renumbered 330-359 in 1926*

C *All fitted with top-covers by 1914, some later fitted with enclosed platforms. Renumbered 360-379 in 1926*

D *Bodies scrapped, electrical gear to new cars with same numbers, 1913-1914*

E *Ex Trafford Park Estates. 162 destroyed in fire 1907, 161 renumbered 151 in 1920s and 380 in 1935. Withdrawn 1947*

F *First cars with top covers, some top covers later removed*

G *Ex Trafford Park Estates. 173 covered top, 173/6 later fitted with enclosed platforms*

H *177 later renumbered 162*

J *Top covers 1923, 151 renumbered 161 in 1920s*

K *Low height cars for working under Gt Ducie St bridge*

L *Top covers fitted 1922*

Buses

Details for several Salford vehicles differ from those in the PSV Circle fleet histories; those in this list have been confirmed from official data and the authors believe them to be correct.

Year	Fleet Nos	Regn Nos	Chassis	Body	Type	Wdn	Note
1920	1	BA 2594	Ld G1	Ld	O45R	1928	
	2	BA 2595	Ld O	EEC	B31R	1929	
1921	3	BA 2597	Ld S5	EEC	B31R	1928	
	4	BA 2596	Ld O	EEC	B31R	1928	
	5	BA 2598	Ld S3	EEC	B33R	1929	E
	6	BA 3025	Ld S5	Ld	B33R	1929	E
	7	BA 2599	Ld O	Ld	B33R	1929	E
	8	BA 3375	Ld O1	Ld	B31R	1928	
1923	9	BA 4008	Vn VSD	Vn	B21F	1928	
	10-11	BA 4147-8	Ld G-	Ld	B32R	1928	
1923/4	12-13	BA 4145-6	Ld G7	EEC	O45R	1928-9	
	14-15	BA 4374-5	Ld G7	Ld	O45R	1929	
	16	BA 4376	Kr K1	Kr	O45R	1929	
1925	17-18	BA 5282-3	Kr JHK	Kr	B31R	1929/31	B
	19	BA 5284	Ld C7	Ld	B32D	1933	
1927	20-21	BA 6264/62	Kr CL6	HL	B20F	1930	
	22-23	BA 6261/63	Kr WL6/1	HL	B32D	1935/31	
	24	BA 6726	Gy FCX	HL	B32D	1931	
	25-36	BA 6735-46	Kr WL6/1	My	B32D	1929-35	
1928	1,4	BA 7015-6	ADC 416A	Hi	B32F	1936	C
	37-42	BA 7295-300	ADC 416A	Dv	B32R	1934-6	
	43-48	BA 7377-82	Kr JKL	Dv	B32R	1934-5	D
	49-54	BA 7383-88	Ds E	Dv	B32R	1937-9	A
	55-60	BA 7389-94	Ld PLSC3	Ld	B32R	1938-9	A

A *3,55-59 scheduled to be renumbered 83-5,92-94 in 1939 but not implemented on the vehicles*
B *18 rebodied by SCT to 26-seat 1929*
C *on hire 3/28 - 7/28*
D *body of 47 fitted to 48 in 10/34*
E *there is conflicting evidence for the withdrawal dates, which may be 1927 or 1928*

Year	Fleet Nos	Regn Nos	Chassis	Body	Type	Wdn	Note
1929	3,9,13/2/4/5,71-9	BA 7670-84	AEC 426	HL	B32D	1937-9	A
	61-70	BA 7685-94	Ds H	HL	L50R	1937-9	
	2	WH 1922	Ld TS1	Bm	C26F	1951	B, C
	5	WH 1442	AEC 426	Bm	B26D	1936	B
	6	WH 1350	TSM B9A	Bu	B35-	1936	B
	7	BN 9999	Ld LTB1	?	C26F	1936	B, D
	8	WH 736	ADC 416D	Dv	B32D	1936	B
	10	WH 380	ADC 417D	?	B26D	1935	B, D

A *14 destroyed in fire, 1929*
B *Ex Tognarelli, Farnworth*
C *new SCT C18R body, 1938 as Salford committee coach & renumbered 402; renumbered 99 1949*
D *Ex Tognarelli, Farnworth; rebuilt by SCT 1930 to B26F*

Year	Fleet Nos	Regn Nos	Chassis	Body	Type	Wdn	Note
1930	11,14,16,17,80-2	BA 8940-6	AEC Re	HL	B32D	1940	A
	83-85	BA 8947-9	Ld TD1	PR	L50R	1939	
	86-91	BA 8950-5	Ds Aw	PR	B31D	1940	A
	92-94	BA 8956/7/39	Ds Le I	PR	L50R	1939	
1932	95-112	RJ 601-18	Ds Le II	Sn	L53R	1937-43	B

A *86-88 seated 32, 11/4/6/7,80-2/6-8 to 31 seat in 1930*
B *seating reduced to 52 circa 1932 and to 48 1936/7*
Note: almost all the subsequent 48 seaters were altered to seat 50 or 54 from 1942 onwards

Year	Fleet Nos	Regn Nos	Chassis	Body	Type	Wdn	Note
1934	18-21/3	RJ 3001-5	Ld TD3	MC	H48R	1949-50	A, D
	24/6/8/30/2	RJ 3006-10	Ld TD3	My	H48R	1948-50	A, C
	36,113	RJ 3011-2	Cy Mn	My	H48R	1946-8	B, D
	114-115	RJ 3013-4	Cy Mn	MC-Cy	H48R	1947-8	B, D
	116-121	RJ 3015-20	AEC Rt 8.8	MC	H48R	1949-51	D

A *9,21,26,28 rebodied Burlingham 1949 and renumbered - see 1949*
B *36,114 new with Gardner 6LW engines; 113 fitted with 6LW engine in 1936, 115 fitted with 6LW engine from 36 in 1946*
C *petrol engines*
D *diesel engines; all subsequent buses are diesel-engined*

Year	Fleet Nos	Regn Nos	Chassis	Body	Type	Wdn	Note
1935	122-130, 22	RJ 3521-30	AEC Rt 8.8	MC	H48R	1949-51	
	25/7/9,31/3	RJ 3531-5	Ld TD4	MC	H48R	1949-50	A, B
	34/5/43/5/6	RJ 3536-40	Ld TD4	My	H48R	1946-51	

A *31/3 rebodied Burlingham in 1949 - see 1949; 46 rebodied Metro Cammell ex 41 in 1947*
B *29 fitted with torque converter transmission, 1936-1947*

Year	Fleet Nos	Regn Nos	Chassis	Body	Type	Wdn	Note
1936	44/7/8, 131/2	RJ 6601-5	Ld TD4	My	H48R	1949	A
	133-142	RJ 6606-15	Ld TD4c	MC	H48R	1949-51	B
	143-152	RJ 6616-25	Ld TD4	MC	H48R	1949-51	
	153-162	RJ 6626-35	AEC Rt 8.8	MC	H48R	1950	

A *44/48,131/2 rebodied Burlingham in 1948/9 - see 1949*
B *135/6/40/2 fitted with crash gearboxes 1947*

Year	Fleet Nos	Regn Nos	Chassis	Body	Type	Wdn	Note
1937	1,4,5	RJ 7001-3	AEC Rl 8.8	EEC	B30R	1950	
	6,7,8	RJ 7004-6	Ld TS7	My	B30R	1950	
	37-42, 163-166	RJ 7007-16	Ld TD4c	MC	H48R	1947-51	C
	167-171	RJ 8711-5	AEC Rl 8.8	EEC	B30R	1950	B
	172-184	RJ 8716-28	AEC Rt 8.8	MC	H48R	1950-51	A
1938	185-196	RJ 8729-40	Ld TD5c	MC	H48R	1950-1	C

A *182-184 had preselector gearboxes and entered service 1938*
B *168 body ex 67 in 1950*
C *37-39,166, 187/9/90-3/6 fitted with crash gearboxes in 1947, 186/8/94/5 in 1948*

1938/9	2,13,49,50,68	ABA 616-20	AEC Rt 8.8	PR	H48R	1951	A
	70/1/3/4/5	ABA 621-5	Ld TD5	Ld	H48R	1951	
	76-78, 197-198	ABA 626-30	Cy Mn	MC	H48R	1950	B, C
	199-208	ABA 631-40	AEC Rt 8.8	MC	H48R	1950-1	C
1939	209-218	ABA 641-50	Ld TD5	MC	H48R	1951	

A 68 destroyed in air raid, 1940
B 77 damaged in accident 1944, chassis scrapped & body to BRJ 901 in 1946
C 76-8, 197-9, 204 entered service 1939

1939	3,9,12/5,51/2/4, 60-2	ARJ 480-9	Ld TD5	MC	H48R	1951	
	63-67	ARJ 490-4	AEC Rl 8.8	EEC	B30R	1950-3	B
	69,72,79,10,106	ARJ 495-9	AEC Rt 8.8	PR	H48R	1950-1	A

A 106 renumbered 100 in 1949
B 67 body to 168 in 1950

1940	53/5-9, 219-227	BBA 538-52	Ld TD5	MC	H48R	1950-2	
	228-232	BBA 553-7	Ld TD5	Ld	H48R	1951	
	233-242	BBA 558-67	AEC Rt 8.8	PR	H48R	1947-51	B
	243-247	BBA 568-72	AEC Rt 8.8	EEC	H48R	1948-51	A

A 247 renumbered 235 in 1950 when 77 (BRJ 901) was renumbered 247
B 234/5 rebuilt to dual-control training buses 1948, renumbered 97/8 1950. To SELNEC, delicensed

1946	1001	TF 9657	Cy Cdr	EEC	H48R		A
	1002	ATC 974	Cy Mn	EEC	H52R		A
	1003-8	VV 3276/8/5/9-81	Cy Mn	MC-Cy	H54R		B
	1009-13	HF 7857/61, HF 8259/61/3	Ld TD2	EEC	H48D	1948	C
	1014	HF 9177	Ld TD3	EEC	H56R	1949	C
	1015	HF 9381	Ld TD3c	Roe	H48C	1947	C
	1016-8	HF 9383/5/91	AEC Rt	EEC	H48D	1949	C
	1019-20	HF 9395/7	AEC Rt	Roe	H52C	1949	C
	77 (247)	BRJ 901	Cy DD42/3	MC	H50R	1962	D

A on hire 11/46-3/47 from Ashton (1001 returned 1/47)
B on hire 11/46 from Northampton, passed to Liverpool 5-8/47
C ex Wallasey Corporation, petrol engined
D Body ex previous 77; fitted with new MC H56R in 1947 & renumbered 247 in 1950

1947	248-262	BRJ 902-16	Cy DD42/3	MC	H56R	1959-62	
	263-277	BRJ 917-31	AEC Rt III	MC	H56R	1962	
	278-295	BRJ 932-49	Ld PD1	MC	H54R	1962	B
	296	BRJ 950	Ld PD1	Ld	H56R	1964	
	297-312	CRJ 297-312	Ld PD1	Ld	H56R	1963-4	
1948	313-342	CRJ 313-342	Ld PD1A	Ld	H56R	1962-4	C
	343-350	CRJ 343-350	Dr CVD6	MC	H56R	1962-3	A

A ordered by Chester Corporation but surplus to their requirements
B 278-281/4 delivered as H50R, altered to 54 in 1949
C cancelled Leyland export order

1948/9	101-110	RJ 6601, 3002, 6603-5, 3534, 3007/8, 3535, 3004	Ld TD	Bm	H56R	1959	A

A Reconditioned chassis with new Burlingham bodies. 107/8 converted to diesel

1950/1	351-440	CRJ 351-440	Dr CVG6	MC	H54R	1963-9	A, B
	441-450	CRJ 441-450	Dr CVG6	Bm	B33R	1959-63	
	451	ERJ 451	Dr CVG6	Bm	FC22F	1962	
1951	452-455	ERJ 452-455	Dr CVG6	Bm	H54R	1966	
1951-2	456-560	FRJ 456-560	Dr CVG6	MC	H54R	1963-9	A

A some to SELNEC
B 351-440/56-560 and subsequent are 8ft (or 8ft 2.5in) wide

1962	101	TRJ 101	AEC Re	Wey	C26F	to SELNEC	
	102-110	TRJ 102-110	AEC Re	Wey	B45F	to SELNEC	
	111-140	TRJ 111-140	Dr CVG6	MC	H65R	to SELNEC	
	141-146	TRJ 141-146	Dr CVG6	MC	H64F	to SELNEC	
1963	147-148	TRJ 147-148	Dr CRG6LX	MC	H74F	to SELNEC	A
1962	149-150	TRJ 149-150	Ld PDR1/1	MC	H77F	to SELNEC	

A later altered to 76 seat

1963	151-188	WRJ 151-188	Ld PD2/40	MC	H64F	to SELNEC	
1964	189-190	ARJ 188-190B	Dr CCG6	MC	H64F	to SELNEC	
	191-205	ARJ 191-205B	Ld PD2/40	MC	H64F	to SELNEC	
	206-208	ARJ 206-208B	Dr CRG6LX	MC	H75F	to SELNEC	
	209-211	ARJ 209-211B	Ld PDR1/1	MC	H77F	to SELNEC	
1965	212-232	DBA 212-232C	Ld PDR1/1	MC	H76F	to SELNEC	
1966	233-257	FRJ 233-257D	Ld PD2/40	MC	H64F	to SELNEC	
1967	258-282	JRJ 258-282E	Ld PD2/40	MC	H64F	to SELNEC	
1968	283-303	MRJ 283-303F	Ld PDR1/1	MC	H77F	to SELNEC	
1969	304-323	PRJ 304-323G	Ld PDR1A/1	PR	H72D	to SELNEC	
1970	(324-343)	SRJ 324-343H	Ld PDR2/1	MC	H78D	to SELNEC	A

A Manchester Mancunian design. Delivered new to SELNEC, numbered 1201-1220

Vehicles to SELNEC

In service: 415/6/8/25/8/9/33/9/57/61/3/5/70/3/8/83/4/5/8/98, 506/7/11/21/2/4/5/7-9/31/3/5-41/3/4/5/7/8/52/3/4/60, 101-323
Withdrawn from service: 97/8, 419/22/58/64/6/7/9/77, 502/8/9/10/2/3/5/26/49/50

CITY OF MANCHESTER

Horse Buses

1-23 (Manchester hackney licences M21-M43) ex Carriage Co L1-23 in 1901, all withdrawn by 1918.
No 2 was preserved by MCT in 1916. It passed to SELNEC and is now in the Museum of Transport

Horse Trams

Carriage Co cars numbered C24-29,31,32,34-36 (two horse, double-deck) were purchased in 1901.
It is *believed* they were numbered 1-11 by Manchester. Scrapped 1903.

Tramcars

Year	Fleet nos	Type	Builder	Body	Wdn	Note
1899	101	4-wheel	MC&T	Open top double-deck	1930	A
	102	4-wheel	HN	Open top double-deck	1928	A
	103	Bogie	Brush	Open top double-deck	1938/9	A
	104	4-wheel	Ashbury	Open top double-deck	1928	A
	105	4-wheel	Milnes	Open top double-deck	1928	A
	106	4-wheel	Milnes	Single deck	1904	A

A Experimental car

Year	Fleet nos	Type	Builder	Body	Wdn	Note
1901/2	107-187	4-wheel	Brush	Open top double-deck	1923-38	
1902/3	188-237	Bogie	Brush	Open top double-deck	1927-1948	
1903	238-276	4-wheel	Brush	Open top double-deck	1923-1938	
1901-3	277-436	4-wheel	Milnes	Open top double-deck	1923-1938	
1901/2	437-486	Bogie	Brush	Open top double-deck	1932-1948	
1903	487-511	4-wheel	Milnes	Open top double-deck	1924-1938	
1903	512-536	Bogie	Milnes	Single deck California car	1928-1935	
1902	537-548	Bogie	Brush	Open top double-deck	1932-1940	
1904-6	549-598	Bogie	Brush	Open top double-deck	1931-1948	
1905/6	599-648	Bogie	Brush	Double deck, open platform	1931-1948	
1907	649-668	Bogie	UEC	Single deck California car	1930	
1909	669-679	4-wheel	Car Wks	Double deck, open platform	1931-8	B
1909-12	680-717	Bogie	Car Wks	Double deck, open platform	1938/9	C
1912/3	718-747	4-wheel	Car Wks	Double deck, open platform	1937-8	B
1913-4	748-762	Bogie	Car Wks	Double deck, open platform	1936-8	B
1914	763-767	Bogie	Car Wks	Single deck California	1930	B
1914-5	768-785	Bogie	Car Wks	Double deck, open platform	1936-8	B
1919	786-792	Bogie	Car Wks	Double deck, open platform	1936-8	B
1920	793-797	Bogie	Car Wks	Double deck, fully enclosed	1939	
1919/20	798-835	Bogie	EEC	Double deck, fully enclosed	1939-47	
1920/1	836-847	Bogie	EEC	Single deck California	1930-1	
1921/2	848-897	Bogie	EEC	Double deck, fully enclosed	1939-48	
1920-2	898-933	Bogie	Car Wks	Double deck, fully enclosed	1939-48	
1925/6	934-993	Bogie	EEC	Double deck, fully enclosed	1945-9	
1925	994-9,529, 1000-1003	Bogie	Brush	Single deck California	1930	A
1927/8	1004-1053	Bogie	EEC	Double deck, fully enclosed	1940-9	

A Ex Middleton, new 1902. Into MCT service 1925-9, 1000-3 not used by MCT

B some parts and sections supplied by Brush;

C 685/6 withdrawn in 1948

REPLACEMENT BUILD

(for accounting reasons these took the numbers of the cars which they replaced)

Year	Fleet nos	Type	Builder	Body	Wdn	Note
1924-30	102/5/8/9/10-4/6/7/9/23/7/8, 134/7-9/47/51/4/7/60/2/4/5/70/1/81-3/4/6/7, 220/38/9/43/5/6/8/51/2/3/9/67/77/8/83/4/9/90/2/4, 309/10/5/9/21/6-8/30/1/6/40/8/52/3/6-8, 360/76/7/9/82/3/8/91/3/4/8, 402/4/6/7/10/7/9/21/2/4/6/7/9/31/2/4/90/1/2/5/7-9, 505/6/11	Bogie	Car Wks	Double deck, fully enclosed	1944-9	

PULLMAN CARS

(for accounting reasons these took the numbers of the cars which they replaced)

Year	Fleet nos	Type	Builder	Body	Wdn	Note
1930-2	104/6/21/5/31/41/4/61/3/73/6/96, 217/25/8/31/42/63/6/70/2/4/87, 349/70/80/1/9, 420/93, 502/3/10/58, 610/69/71/6	4-wheel	Car Wks	Double deck, fully enclosed	1946-8	A

A All sold for further service to Leeds (7), Sunderland (6), Aberdeen (14) and Edinburgh (11)

Buses

Year	Fleet Nos	Registration No	Chassis	Body	Seats	Wdn	Note
1906	1-3	N 1593, 1601/2	Ld Y	Dick Kerr	O33R	1909-13	
1908-9	4,3	N 3635, 4587	Ryknield R	Dick Kerr	O33R	1913	
1913	1-4	N 9245-7, 9302	Dr CC	Dodson	O33R	1914	A
1914	5-8	N 9803-5, NA557	Dr CC	Brush	O33R	1914	B
1915	9-11	NA 2687/8/92	Dr Y	Car Wks	O38R	1924	

A N9246/302 chassis requisitioned by War Department, bodies to store

B Chassis requisitioned by War Department, bodies to store

Fleet numbers *From 1916 until April 1927 fleet numbers were not used - the registration number being used for identification. The fleet numbers shown in the list hereafter are the series introduced in 1927.*

Year	Fleet Nos	Registration No	Chassis	Body	Seats	Wdn	Note
1916	1-3, –, 5-6	NA 6623-8	Dr Y	note A	O33R	1925-8	A, C
1919	9	NB 1924	Dr Y	note A	O33R	1927-8	A
	–, 6	NB 2167/2254	AEC YC	BCLE	O33R	1919/27	
	7	NB 2355	AEC YC	Car Wks	O39R	1927	
	8	NB 2669	AEC YC	note A	O33R	1927	A
1921	9	NB 3741	Dr Y	note A	O33R	1921	B

A Bodies ex store, previously fitted to the 1913/4 chassis requisitioned by War Department

B converted to lorry

C 1-5 were NA6623-5/7-8, NA6626 withdrawn 1925

1922	10-11	NC 5666-7	AEC S	Fry	O54R	1928-9	
	–	NC 7911	Kr H	Kr	B20F	1923	A

A - returned to Karrier in exchange for one of the 1923 CY

1923	12-15	ND 2272-4/6	Kr CY	Kr	B20F	1928-9	
	–	ND 2777-8	Vn	Vn	B20F	1927	
1924	16-21	ND 4399/400/54/511, ND 5291, 5763	Kr JH	HL	B30F	1928	A
	22-27	ND 6234-7, 8183, 8201	Bl 4-ton	Bl	B30F	1930	

A *body possibly by Strachan & Brown*

1925	28-37	ND 9278-80/668/9/51, NE 312-5	AEC 401	Dv	O54R	1929-30	
	–	BU 1412/3	AEC YB	–	B--F	1926	A
	38	HO 5506	Dr Y	–	B32F	1927	B
	39-46	NE 436/7,744,942/76, NE 1410/36/98	Kr JHS	SB	B30R	1928-9	
	47	NE 4660	Dr CL	SB	B30R	1931	

A *ex Middleton, new 1920; withdrawn before fleet numbers allocated in 1927*
B *ex Middleton, new 1921*

1926	48-56	NE 7867-9, 8101/629/30, NE 9338/9/82	Dr CL	SB	B30R	1929-31	A
1927	57-59	NF 1802-4	Dr 36CM	Dv	B30F	1930-1	
	60-65	NF 4078-80/143-5	Bl A	Bl	H52R	1935	
	66-68	NF 4168, 4300-1	Ld PLSP1	Ld	H52R	1931-4	
	69	NF 7810	Bl B	Bl	B32R	1937	
	70-71	NF 7811/47	ADC 416D	Dv	B32R	1931	
	72	NF 7848	Kr WL6/2	RSJ	H65R	1933	
	73-76	NF 8037/8/91/121	ADC 416D	Dv	B32R	1931-2	
	77-89	NF 8143/82/233/58/9, NF 8313/82/434/5/85-8	Bl B	Bl	B32R	1936-7	
	90-98	NF 8555/8/9/654/704-8	ADC 416D	LGOC	B32R	1932-4	
	99	NF 8709	Bl B	Bl	B32R	1937	

A *Edinburgh" cut-away rear platform introduced*

1928	100-113	PT 4701-5/8/11/2/4/8/20-3	Bl 4-ton	RSJ	B26D	1929-31	A
	114-125	VM 1965/6/2491/2/646/7 VM 2793/932,3254-6	Bl B	Bl	B32R	1935-7	
	126-137	VM 3257,4442-4, 5313-20	ADC 423	Dv	B32R	1936	
	(38)	VM 3675	Cy Eagle	Dv	B32R	1934	B
	138-140	VM 4439-4441	Ld TS1	Dv	B32R	1949	C

A *Ex Sunderland District via Wintour, dealer, to allow withdrawal of the Karriers; new 1924*
B *Crossley's first full size bus, on hire; purchased 9/28 and numbered 7/29*
C *Rebodied MC-Cy B32R 1935*

1929	141-143	VM 6401-3	Ds E	Dv	B32R	1934	
	144-148	VM 6404-8	Cy Eagle	Dv	B32R	1934	
	41	WH 275	ADC 417D	Wk	B26D	1931	A, B
	42	WH 476	ADC 416D	Dv	B32D	1931	A
	43	WH 735	ADC 416	Dv	B32D	1931	A
	44	WH 1351	AEC 426	Bell	B32F	1934	A
	45	WH 1161	Ld TS1	Bm	B26D	1940	A, C, G
	46	WH 1921	Ld TS2	Bm	C26D	1940	A, B, C, G
	149-158	VR 2627, 4149/51/252/1/3-7	Cy Six	Cy	B32R	1937-9	E, F
1929/30	159-163	VR 4573/776/5/52/1	Cy Six	Car Wks	B32R	1937-9	

A *ex Tognarelli, Farnworth, new 1927-9*
B *rebuilt to B32R at once*
C *rebuilt to B31F at once*
D *new Car Wks B32R 1933 (46), 1936 (45)*
E *149 used as committee coach*
F *150 burnt out in fatal fire 11/33, rebodied Car Wks to original design and renumbered 7*
G *45/46 (along with fleet numbers 9,12,16,18,19,21) were ARP ambulances during the war*

STANDARD DESIGN - "PIANO FRONT"

Buses 189-389. Corresponding design for single-deckers

1930	164-173	VR 4572/1/750/47/9/8, VR 4868-71	Cy Six	Cy	B32R	1937-9	A
	174-188	VR 7530-4, 8549-52, VR 9164-6, 9668-70	Cy Six	Car Wks	B32R	1937-9	
	28/9,31/3-5	VR 5742, 5994-8	Ld TS2	Car Wks	B32R	1940	B
	189-198	VR 6008-14, 6683-5	Cy Cdr	Cy	L50R	1937-46	
	199-204	VR 6686-90,7538	Cy Cdr	Arnold	L50R	1939-46	
	205-208	VR 7535-7/9	Cy Cdr	Brush	L50R	1938-46	
	209-224	VR 5764-6,6001-7, VR 6681/2, 6017-20	Ld TD1	Brush	L50R	1949	C
	225-236	VR 5258/469-71/749-56	Ld TD1	Short	L50R	1949-50	D
	237-248	VR 5472/757-63/7/8, 6015/6	Ld TD1	Sn	L50R	1949-50	E
	8-22	VU 341-3/7/8,625-34	Cy Six	Car Wks	B32R	1937-40	F
	30,100-113	VR 9662-7/71-6, VU 344-6,	Ld TS2	Vn	B32R	1944-6	B, G
	249-278	VU 349-50, 636-44/35, VU 766-783	Cy Cdr	Cy	L50R	1937-47	H, J

A *164/5 entered service 12/29*
B *rebuilt Car Wks B32R 1937-9 (essentially rebody to original design), most were ambulances during war. 33 reinstated 1945, withdrawn 1948*
C *221 burnt out on loan to Crosville, 1945*
D *233 burnt out on loan to Crosville, 1945*
E *238/41 withdrawn 1947/1943 after crash*
F *20-22 new 1/31*
G *111 to ambulance 1940, 100 scrapped by MCT 1944 after crash on loan to Braithwaite, Stockton*
H *269-277 new 1931. 264 scrapped after accident, 1934*
J *278 had a Gardner 6L2 diesel engine*

1931	279-318	VU 3627-3666	Cy Cdr	Cy	H52R	1937-46	
	319	VU 3667	Dr CH6	E&K	H52R	1937	B
	320	VU 3668	Cy Cdr	Cy	L50R	1947	A
	321-324	VU 6287-90	Cy Cdr	Car Wks	H48R	1939-46	C
	325-330	VU 6291-6	Cy Cdr	Car Wks	H52R	1937-46	

A New 1930 as Cy diesel prototype; renumbered 264 5/37 into lowbridge series
B Eastwood & Kenning, Trafford Park took over the bankrupt Davidson business
C diesel engine

All subsequent new motor buses were diesel-engined, other than coach 6 (BVU98)

1932	331-350	VU 7394-7413	Cy Cdr	Sn	H50R	1946-50	A
	351-360	VU 7414-7423	Cy Cdr	Car Wks	H51R	1940-50	B

A 331-7 new 1931
B 356 seated 50

1933	361-370	XJ 2240-9	Cy Cdr	Car Wks	H52R	1940-50	
1932	371-380	XJ 2250-9	Cy Cdr	Cy	H52R	1940-9	
1932/3	381-389	XJ 2260-8	Cy Cdr	HN	H52R	1940-9	A
1932	390	XJ 2269	Cy Cdr	MC	H52R	1950	B
1933	39	VU 392	Cy Eagle	Cy	B32R	1934	C
	–	LG 2617	AEC Rl	–	–	–	C, D
	(40)	VR 9810	Cy Eagle	Cy	B32R	–	C, D
	–	VU 425	AEC Rl	–	–	–	C, D
	391-400	XJ 9270-4, ANA 227,724 ANA 814, ANB 76, ANC 139	Cy Cdr	Car Wks	H52R	1940-50	E

A 381-5 new 1932
B 390 was the metal-framed "Standard" prototype
C Ex Sykes, Sale; new 1930
D sold at once
E Bodies of Piano-front style but with "Standard" style sloping front; 400 new 1934

STANDARD DESIGN - THE "STANDARD"

401-550/64-600, 23-27, 36/7, 47-59 have all-metal framed "Standard" design bodies.

1934	401-405	ANB 470, AND 203, ANF 971, ANE 70, AVR 386	Cy Cdr	MV-Car Wks	(A)	1948-9	A
1933	406-415	XJ 7980, 8559-62, 9027-31	Cy Cdr	MV-Cy	H56R	1947-50	B
	416-420	XJ 7706-7710	Ld TD2	MC	H56R	1951	C

A Lightweight alloy frames by Metropolitan Vickers. 401/2 were H56R, 403-5 were H55R. 401 new 12/33
B Lightweight alloy frames by Metropolitan Vickers
C bodies ex 272, 275, 271, 293, 314 in 1946-9

1934	421-435	AND 16-30	Cy Mn	MC	H54R	1948-50	
	436-465	ANB 851, 13, 852-5, ANC 673/81, ANC 822-3, ANC 682, 824, 674, ANC 683,825/6, AND 90/1,198/9,92/3, AND 200, 94, 201/2, ANE 71-4	Cy Mn	A&P-Cy	H56R	1948-50	
	466-500	AVM 151-61, 331, 162, AVM 332/0/3/4, AVR 281, AVM 833-5, AVR 282, AVM 831, AVR 751, AVM 832, AVR 284-6/3/7/8, 752-5	Cy Mn	MC-Cy	H54R	1947-50	
	71 (320)	AXJ 77	Cy 6-wheel	MV-Car Wks	H63R	1946	A

A ex-Crossley intended demonstrator; chassis was a hybrid Condor/Mancunian. Bought by MCT as chassis and body frame in 4/33, body finished in Car Works apprentice school. Renumbered 320 5/37

1934/5	501-520	AXJ 475/6, 970-987	Cy Mn	MC-Cy	H52R	1948-50	A
	521-530	AXJ 793/4, 477/8, 856-61	Ld TD3	MC	H54R	1951-4	B
	23-27, 36/7, 47-59	AXJ 304, 257, 460/1, AXJ 305, 462/3 AXJ 306, 464-6, 307, AXJ 467-74	Cy Mn	MC-Cy	B32R	1943-9	

A 501 had a Wilson pre-selector gearbox when new. Replaced by Freeborn fully automatic gearbox, 8/36. In 10/36 this was replaced by a standard crash box, the body was removed to allow this and was fitted to 577 new, the new H54R body built for 577 was then fitted to 501
B rebodied as follows - ex 525, 1332, 911, 521, 528, 527, 523, 529, 1319 in 1947, 1942, 1946, 1947, 1946, 1948, 1946, 1946 and 1945 respectively; 530 was the only one which retained its own body, which was rebuilt in 1947

1935	6	BVU 98	Cy Delta	Cy	C20F	1946	A
1935/6	531-545	BVU 667-681	Cy Mn	MC-Cy	H56R	1949-51	

A Airport coach, petrol engined; unique vehicle

1936	(39)	VR 8766	AEC Re	Short	B30-	at once	A
	(40)	MY 638	AEC Re	Short	B32F	at once	A
	(41)	VR 7189	Cy Six	Roe	B32-	at once	A
	(42)	MP 3272	ADC 416	LGOC	B---	at once	A
	43	VM 7166	AEC 426	HL	B32R	1936	A

A ex Sharp, Longsight, new 1930, 1929, 1930, 1930, 1929 respectively

REBODYING with STANDARD bodies
to replace the timber-framed bodies which were coming to the end of their planned life

1934	Cy composite L52R	199,201-4, 255; 272 (after accident)
1935/6	MC-Cy L52R	189-93/5/7 200/5/8 209-248 249-51/3/6/9-63/5-9/71/3-7/84. 320
	MC-Cy H52R	307 (after accident)
	MC-Cy B32R	138-140
1936/7	MC-Cy H56R	194/6/8 206/7, 252/4/7/8/70/8/87/93/6, 310/21
	MC-Cy H54R	331/3-9/41-4/7/8/52/5

Displaced bodies from 333/7/42/55 overhauled and fitted to 300, 294/2/83

RENUMBERING

After rebodying there were 11 fewer lowbridge buses and to bring all highbridge fleet numbers above 268, pairs of buses exchanged numbers in 1936/7

Highbridge bus	Lowbridge bus	Highbridge bus	Lowbridge bus
194 became 284	284 became 194	196 became 271	271 became 196
198 became 274	274 became 198	206 became 269	269 became 206
207 became 272	272 became 207	252 became 275	275 became 252
254 became 276	276 became 254	257 became 273	273 became 257
258 became 277	277 became 258	320 became 264	264 scrapped after accident

REBODYING with STANDARD bodies
to replace the Accles and Pollock framed bodies,
which were then overhauled and placed on earlier chassis

1937/8	MC-Car Works H54R	437-9/41-61/5
1938/9	Cy-Car Works H54R	436/40/62-4

20 of the displaced bodies overhauled and fitted to 279-282, 285 (two bodies), 286/8/90/1/7/8, 302/4/8/9/11/2/5/6

LOWBRIDGE BODIES (with their fleet numbers) moved to later chassis
to provide more lowbridge diesels for the 53 service

1937-1939	332/40/6/9/50/6/7/8/64/8/70/5/7 fitted with body from and renumbered to 249, 191, 189, 259, 195, 256, 190, 193, 263, 194 (originally 284), 205, 200, 251

STANDARD DESIGN - STREAMLINER

546 onwards were ordered as Streamliners, for speed of delivery 546-550 and 564-600 were built as Standards. 602-1361 were Streamliners. The single deck Mancunians and TS8s were also Streamliners.

1936/7	546-550	CNF 560-564	Cy Mn	MC-Cy	H54R	1951-3	
	551-558	CVR 753-760	Cy Mn	MC-Cy	H52R	1952-3	
	559-563	CXJ 928, DNB 46/7,723/4	Cy Mn	EEC-Cy	H50R	1953-4	A
	564-600	CVM 535-7, CVR 36, CVM 844-6, CVR 37-40, CVU 328/9/32, CXJ 929, CVU 330, CVR 41, CVU 333, DNA 455/6, CVU 331, CXJ 927, DNB 42-5, 725-8, DNC 104-7, 139-141	Cy Mn	MC-Cy	H54R	1950-3	B
	601	CXJ 930	Cy Mn	Cy	H52R	1951	

A *560 wrecked in accident 1948*

B *577 body ex 501 when new*

1937	602-607	DNA 451-4, CXJ 932/1	Ld TD4	MC-Cy	H54R	1951	A
	608-614	DND 921-6, DNE 648	Cy Mn	MC-Cy	H52R	1950-1	
	126-137, 141-148	DNF 201-9/17-9, DNF 220, DVM 511-7	Cy Mn	MC-Cy	B32R	1948-50	
	615-627	DNE 649-653, DNF 210-6, DVM 518	Cy Mn	MC-Cy	H54R		
	628-634	DVR 600, DVU 190/1, 572, DXJ 300/1, 659	Cy Mn	EEC-Cy	H52R	1950-1	
	635-642	DVU 939-945, DVR 601	Ld TD5	MC-Cy	H54R	1951-3	

A *607 seated 52*

1937/8	60-99	DXJ 302/14, DVU 11,573, DXJ 313, DVU 936, 12, DXJ 303/15, DVU 13, 574, DXJ 316, DVU 937, DXJ 317, DVU 575/6, DXJ 318, DVU 577/8,938, DXJ 304-7/19, DVU579/80, DXJ 308, DVU 946/7, DXJ 309, 653, 310, DXJ 654-6, 311, DXJ 657/8, 312	Ld TS8	MC-Cy	B32R	1951-4	A, B, C, D, E
	643-710	DVM 519-22, DVR248-53, DVR 596-9, DVU14-6, DXJ 660-7, ENA 357-68, ENA 716-24, ENB 423-8, ENB 906-11/3/4, ENC 322-6, 933-5	Cy Mn	MC-Cy	H54R	1949-51	F, G

A *60 rebuilt Bond C30F for airport 1950; 64 rebuilt Car Wks C20R for airport, 1946*

B *71 rebuilt Car Wks normal control B26F 1949 for 110 service*

C *78/9 rebuilt Car Wks-Stockport Mfg Co C20R for airport 1949*

D *89 rebuilt Bond C30F 1950 for airport; 97/9 rebuilt County, Leigh C30F for airport 1950*

E *98 rebuilt MC C20R for airport, 1946*

F *657 destroyed by fire in accident 2/40. Rebuilt fitted with new chassis and new Car Wks H56R body and re-registered GNC788 in 1940. Body ex 278 in 1949*

G *710 wrecked in accident inside Hyde Road garage, 1948*

1938	1000-1027	DXJ 951-978	Cy TDD4	MC-Cy	H54R	1953-6	A
	1028-1037	DXJ 979-988	Ld TB4	MC-Cy	H54R	1954-5	A, B
	1050-1061	DXJ 989-993, ENB 175-181	Cy TDD6	MC-Cy	H68R	1950-6	A
	1062-1087	ENB 182-207	Ld TTB4	MC-Cy	H68R	1950-6	A
	711-722	ENB 912, ENC 327, 936, ENB 915, ENC 937-44	Cy Mn	MC-Car Wks	H54R	1950-4	

A *Trolleybuses*

B *1033 withdrawn 1951*

1938/9	723-750	EVM 974/5, EVR 349-52, EVR 736-41,EVU 256-61, FNA 49-52, 276-81	Cy Mn	MC-Car Wks	H54R	1951-7	
	751-782	EVR 732-5/42/3, EVU 254/5, FNA 47, EVU 879/80, FNA 48, EVM 964-73, EVR 353-60, FVM 311/2	Cy Mn	MC-Cy	H54R	1951-6	A, B
1938	783-802	EVU 250-3, 517-28, 869-72	Ld TD5	MC-Cy	H54R	1956-61	
	803-814	EVU 320-31	Ld TD5	Ld	H54R	1953-60	C

A *781/2 were built with 970-999 in 1939.*
B *773 wrecked in accident, fitted with new chassis and body 1939, original body rebuilt and fitted to new chassis 988*
C *813 rebodied EEC H54R ex 1323 after accident 1946*

1939	815-826	FNA 455-7, FNB 666-74	Cy Mn	MC-Car Wks	H54R	1954-7	A
	827-836	FNC 511-20	Cy Mn	MC-Car Wks	H54R	1953-7	B
	837-861	FNC 220-31, 510	Cy Mn	MC-Cy	H54R	1953-7	C, D, E
	862-886	FNA 334-358	Ld TD5	Ld	H54R	1956-9	F
	887-936	FND 869—888, FNF 807-15, FVM 10-3/5-20/2-32	Ld TD5	Ld	H55R	1957-62	G, H, J
	937-938	FXJ 318-9	Ld TD5	Cy	H54R	1959/61	K

A *All fitted with Gardner 5LW engines, 1944-5*
B *827/31/3/5 fitted with Gardner 5LW engines, 1944-5*
C *All except 848, 851 fitted with Gardner 5LW engines, 1944-6*
D *840/3/4/61 fitted with Cy engines 1950-1*
E *838 rebodied MC-Cy H56R Standard ex 287 after crash in Queens Rd garage 1948*
F *867/76-86 seated 55*
G *914 withdrawn 1953 after accident*
H *922/3 fitted with Ld 7.4 litre engines 1948 and 1951 respectively*
J *911 body badly damaged in accident 1944. Fitted with EEC H54R built for 1320 in 1946, Leyland body rebuilt and fitted to 523*
K *all-Cy body*

REBODYING with CAR WORKS COMPOSITE interim-life bodies

1939-42	Car Wks H56R	284 (formerly 194), 278/9/88/97, 304/8/12/5/51/65, 401/2/4/5/6/8/10-5, 657

414 received two bodies, its first being destroyed by fire before re-entering service

1939/40	939-969	FXJ 320-2, 973-982, GNA 161-70, 401-8	Ld TD5	MC-Cy	H54R	1958-62	A
1939	970-999	FNC 521, FND 889-92, FNF 804-6, FVM 33-36, FVM 306-10/3-25	Cy Mn	MC-Cy	H54R	1954-7	B, C, D
1939	1200-1216	FXJ 63-72, 311-7	Cy Mn	MC-Cy	H54R	1953-6	E
	1217-1253	–	Cy Mn	MC-Cy	H54R	–	F

A *939/40 new 12/39*
B *988 new with rebuilt body ex accident damaged 773*
C *986 scrapped 1950 after crash. All fitted with Gardner 5LW engines, 1942-4*
D *997 MCT's last Mancunian in service withdrawn 5/57*
E *1211 body to 1217 1944, new Cy H54R body built for 1217 fitted*
F *not delivered due to redirection of Crossley to military vehicle production. Their body frames were completed by Metro Cammell and were modified to fit Daimler chassis. 23 were then finished by Crossley and fitted to 1254-1276. There were no more COG5 chassis available due to the bombing of Daimler's works and the other 14 frames were sent to Weymann, finished to utility standards on Guy chassis and allocated to Newport (2), BMMO (2), Sheffield (5), Midland General (2) and Coventry (3)*

1940/1	1100-1136	GNA 18-54	Ld TB5	EEC	H54R	1954-9	N
1940	1137-1176	GNA 55-94	Cy TDD4	MC-Cy	H54R	1954-60	N,P,R
1940/1	1254-1276	GNB 496, GNC 53, GNB 497-9, GNC 57/8/4-6/9-64, GNC102-7/10	Dr COG5	MC-Cy	H54R	1958-62	A, M
	1277-1286	(GNC 108/9/11-18)	Dr COG5	MC-Cy	–	–	F, K, M
	1287-1316	GNA 435-64	Dr COG5	EEC	H54R	1954-59	
	1317-1322	(GNB 102-7)	Dr COG5	EEC	–	–	G
	1323-5, 1329/31	GNB 108/9, 460/3/5	Dr COG5	EEC	H54R	1957-8	D
	1326-8/30 1332-40	(GNB 110,461-2/4/6-74)	Dr COG5	EEC	–	–	G
	1341-1344	GNB 475-478	Dr COG5	EEC	H54R	1955-7	B, D
	1345/6 1351/2/4/5	(GNB 479/80/5/6/8/9)	Dr COG5	EEC	–	–	G
	1347-50/3	GNB 481-4/7	Dr COG5	EEC	H54R	1956/7	B, C, D
	1356-1361	GNB 490-5	Dr COG5	EEC	H54R	1956-9	E, L
	1362-1369	–	Dr COG5	Cy	–	–	H
	1370-1402	GNA 409/10, 556-565, GNA 667-676, GNB 1-10, 101	Ld TD5	MC-Cy	H54R	1954-62	E
	1403-1436	–	Cy Mn	MC-Cy	–	–	J, K

A *1273 rebodied EEC H54R intended for 1345; 1266 last pre-war vehicle in fleet, withdrawn 9/62 as 4266*
B *1343 body completed by MCT; 1344 body fitted by MCT;1350 body completed and fitted by MCT*
C *1348/50 chassis assembled from several damaged ones; 1349 body fitted by MCT*
D *chassis of 1323-5/44/9 recovered part-built from the blitzed Daimler works, brought to Manchester and completed in the Car Works by MCT*
E *1358 (as 4358) withdrawn 1953 after crash, 1372/5 (as 3372/5) withdrawn 1954*
F *not delivered due to war bombing of Daimler factory*
G *chassis not delivered due to war bombing of Daimler factory, EEC bodies delivered - those for 1319/20/28/32/45 used by MCT on 529, 911,1323, 522, 1273; the remaining bodies were sold to Birmingham*
H *not delivered due to war bombing of Daimler factory*
J *not delivered due to redirection of Crossley to military vehicle production*
L *1358 withdrawn 1953 after accident*
M *intended to have Crossley bodies which were not built due to redirection of Crossley to military vehicle production. Instead the Metro Cammell frames built for Crossleys 1217-1239 were modified to fit COG5 chassis, finished by Crossley and fitted to 1254-1276. See note under 1217-1253*
N *Trolleybuses*
P *1147-53/6/9/63 stored until 1941, 1167-71 built 1941, 1172-4 part built 1941and completed by Crossley 1942, 1175/6 part built 1941and completed by Crossley 1943 and 1944*
R *1139 withdrawn 1953*

1944	1217	GNE 247	Cy DD42/1	MC-Cy	H54R	1963	

Prototype postwar chassis, body ex 1211, body intended for 1217 fitted to 1211; on loan to MCT 5/44-7/47 then purchased. Fitted at various times with turbo-transmitter transmission, fitted with Ld 8.6 litre engine and gearbox 1952

1944	114-115	DK 7380-7381	Ld TS1	Bm	C32F	1946/5	A, B
	394 (3601)	DDK 441	Ld TD5	Bm	H56R	1951	A, C

A Ex Yelloway with the Rochdale - Royton - Manchester service, joint purchase with Rochdale and Oldham Corporations, new 1931, 1931, 1938 respectively

B Sent immediately on loan to Sutton, Kidsgrove and sold to them without ever running for MCT

C Allocated number 3782 in 1946 but not implemented. Body scrapped 1947 and replaced by MC Standard ex 524, renumbered 3601

1945/6	4200-4242	GNB 461-2/4/6-4/9, GNB 480/5/6/8/9, GNF 155-179	Dr CWA6	Brush	H56R	1950-2	A

A Relaxed utility bodies, the chassis were the balance of the order for 116 COGs, using the issued but not used registration numbers. 4200/2/5 new 12/45

RENUMBERING - the "thousands" scheme

Implemented from 1945 (but not completed until 1951 with 529) this grouped vehicles into "thousand" blocks by make or type. Most vehicles had the appropriate "thousand" added to the fleet number (replacing the 1xxx digit in the case of the Daimler COG5s and Leylands 1370-1402) and only the following needed to be renumbered: 1200-1216 to 2870 - 2886, 1217 to 2887 then 2960 (2887 not carried), 1370-1402 to 3370-3402, 394 to 3782 (never carried) then 3601

MCT "Postwar Standard" body

Fitted to 2890-2959/61-2, 3000-3264, 2000-2108, 2110-2219, 4000-4099. Except for 2890-2959/61-2, all subsequent vehicles are of 8ft or 8ft 2.5in width

1946/7	2890 -2959/61	GNF 820-890	Cy DD42/3	Cy	H56R	1962-3	A, B, C, D, E

A 2954-9 fitted with turbo-transmitter transmission; Ld 8.6 litre engine and gearbox 1953/4

B 2891-4/6/7/8/900-2/22/3 fitted with Ld 8.6 litre engine ex withdrawn TD1s 1949-50,

C 2890/5/9 exchanged numbers with 2922/02/23 to bring the Ld engined buses into the block 2890-2901

D 2948/52-9/61 seated 58; 2937 had platform doors

E 2961 intended to be numbered 2960, altered before delivery to enable the former 1217 to become 2960 next to the other turbo-transmitter buses.

1947/8	2000-2108	GVR 93-110/2-201, HVM 621	Cy DD42/4	Cy	H58R	1964-6	
1947	3000-3049	GVR 202-251	Ld PD1/1	MC	H58R	1963-6	
	3050-3099	GVR 252-301	Ld PD1/3	MC	H58R	1965-8	
	4050-4099	GVR 352-401	Dr CVG5	Brush	H58R	1965-8	
1948	2962	JND 964	Cy DD42/5	Cy	H58R	1963	A
1948/9	2110-2141	JND 751-782	Cy DD42/4	Cy	H58R	1965-6	
	2142-2159	JND 783-800	Cy DD42/8S	Cy	H58R	1966-7	B

A Ordered as mobile library by City Libraries Committee, exchanged for pre-war Crossley single-deckers fleet nos. 49 and 55

B 2152-9 had platform doors; 2158 withdrawn 1964; 2143/5/7 fitted with 5LW engines, 1956

1949	2160-2219	GVR 111, KNA 601-659	Cy DD42/8S	Cy	H58R	1964-5	B, C
	3100-3199	JNA 401-500	Ld PD1/3	MC	H58R	1966-9	
	4000-4049	GVR302-351	Dr CVG5	Cy	H58R	1965-8	C

A 4034 dismantled after crash, 1951

B 2160 registered GVR111 in error, changed to NVU 137 6/54; 2214-9 had saloon heaters

C 2172/82/9/98, 2203 fitted with 5LW engines 1953, 1956, 1954, 1959, 1960 respectively

1949/50	1200-1237	JVU 707-744	Cy TDD42/1	Cy	H58R	1963	A
1951	1240-1255	JVU 745-760	Cy TDD64/1	Cy	H66R	1963	A
1951/2	3200-3264	JND 601-665	Ld PD2/3	MC	H58R	3224 1969, rest to SELNEC	
1950	3265-3299	JND 666-700	Ld PD2/3	Ld	H58R	1968/9, some to SELNEC	
1950/1	4100-4189	JND 701-750	Dr CVG6	MC	H58R	1968-9, some to SELNEC	B

A trolleybuses

B 4149 dismantled after crash, 1966; 4175-7 5LW engines during 1952-3 only

1953	1-18	NNB 101-118	Ld PSU1/13	NC	B42R	1967-8	
	20-23	NNB 120-123	Ld PSU1/13	NC	B43F	1968	A
	24-25	NNB 124-125	Ld PSU1/13	NC	B33C	1966/3	B
	30-32	NNB 130-132	Ld PSU1/13	Bond	RC41F	1967	C
	33-35	NNB 133-135	Ld PSU1/13	Bm	RC41F	1967-8	C
1953/4	3300-3329	NNB 140-169	Ld PD2/12	NC	H60R	1968-9, one to SELNEC	D
	3330-3369	NNB 170-209	Ld PD2/12	Ld	H60R	19 in 1968, rest to SELNEC	F
	4400-4479	NNB 210-289	Dr CVG6K	MC	H60R	all to SELNEC	
1955	4480-4489	NNB 290-299	Dr CVG6K	MC	H61R	all to SELNEC	E

A one-man operated

B centre-entrance "crush-loader"; 24 carried 26 standing and 25 carried 24 standing; both altered to B41C 1958

C raised-roof airport coaches; 30-32 had Burlingham frames

D 3323-5/7-9 seated 61

E 4488 fitted with 5LW engine 1955; 4480-9 lightweight bodies, standard weight chassis.

F 3363 withdrawn 1966 after crash, body to 3494

1955/6	1301-1362	ONE 701-762	BUT 9612T	Bm	H60R	1964/6	A, B
1956	3411-3470	PND 411-470	Ld PD2/12	MC	H64R	to SELNEC	
1955	4490	PND 490	Dr CVG5K	MC	H64R	to SELNEC	D
	4491-4509	PND 491-509	Dr CVG5K	MC	H64R	to SELNEC	
1956	36-39	NNB 136-139	Ld PSUC1/1T	Bm	RC41F	1969	C
1956/7	4510-4549	RND 510-549	Dr CVG5K	NC	H64R	to SELNEC	E

A trolleybuses

B 1346 scrapped 1962 after accident

C Registration numbers "in stock" since 1953

D lightweight chassis

E lightweight bodies

1958	3471-3514	TNA 471-514	Ld PD2/40	Bm	H65R	to SELNEC	A
1958	3515-3520	TNA 515-520	Ld PD2/34	Bm	H65R	to SELNEC	B
1957/8	4550-4579	TNA 550-579	Dr CVG6K	Bm	H65R	to SELNEC	D
1958	40-45	UXJ 240-245	An MR11L	Seddon	B40F	1968	C

A 3494 rebodied Ld body ex 3363, 10/66;
B Semi-automatic gearboxes, 3520 fully automatic
C Licensed as Leyland MR11L
D 4552 fitted with Gardner 6LX engine, 1961-1964

1958/9	3521-3620	UNB 521-620	Ld PD2/40	MC	H65R	to SELNEC	A
1959	3621-3630	UNB 621-630	Ld PDR1/1	MC	H77F	to SELNEC	B

A 3581/2 had Cave-Browne-Cave heating systems; B - 3629/30 had air suspension, removed 1964/5

1961	4580-4589	9580-9589 NA	Dr CVG6K	MC	H65R	to SELNEC	B
	46-50	9746-9750 NA	Ld PSUC1/2	PR	DP40F	to SELNEC	
	3631-3670	9831-9870 NA	Ld PD2/37	MC	H65R	to SELNEC	
1962	51-54	3651-3654 NE	Ld PSUC1/2	PR	DP36F	to SELNEC	A
	55-60	3655-3660 NE	Ld PSUC1/2	PR	DP38D	to SELNEC	A
1963	3671-3695	3671-3695 NE	Ld PD2/37	MC	H65R	to SELNEC	
1962/3	4590-4609	4590-4609 NE	Dr CRG6LX	MC	H76F	to SELNEC	

A blue livery for airport work
B 4588/9 had Daimatic semi-automatic gearboxes

1963/4	4610-4629	4610-4629 VM	Dr CRG6LX	MC	H76F	to SELNEC	A
1963	4630-4649	4630-4649 VM	Dr CVG6K	MC	H65R	to SELNEC	
	4650-4654	4650-4654 VM	Dr CCG6K	MC	H65R	to SELNEC	
1964	3696-3720	889 VU, 3697-3720 VM	Ld PD2/37	MC	H65R	to SELNEC	
	4655-4684	ANA 655-684B	Dr CGR6LX	MC	H76F	to SELNEC	
1964/5	61-80	ANF 161/2B BND 863-880C	Ld PSRC1/1R	PR	B43D	to SELNEC	B

A 4628 was built new with the prototype wrap-around windscreen
B 71-80 fitted new with turbochargers, disconnected after a few months.

1965	3721-3792	BND 721-792C	Ld PDR1/2	MC	H76F	to SELNEC	
1965-7	4701-4760	DNF 701-730C FNE 731-760D	Dr CRG6LX	MC	H76F	to SELNEC	
1966	3801-3860	END 801-860D	Ld PDR1/2	MC	H76F	to SELNEC	
1967	81-99, 101-110	GND 81-99E GND 101-110E	Ld PSUR1/1R	MC	B40D	to SELNEC	A
1966/7	201/3/5	GNB 516-518D	Bd VAL14	Pn	C47F	to SELNEC	C
	202/4/6	GND 111-113E	Bd VAL14	Pn	C47F	to SELNEC	B, C

A bus 100 destroyed in fire at MCW and not replaced
B 203 C45F
C white and turquoise coach livery

***STANDARD DESIGN - MANCUNIAN** all subsequent double-deckers are Mancunians*

1968	1001-1048	HVM 901-948F	Ld PDR1/1	PR	H73D	to SELNEC	
	2001-2048	HVM 801-848F	Dr CRG6LX	PR	H73D	to SELNEC	
	207-212	JND 207-212F	Bd VAL70	Pn	C52F	to SELNEC	
1968/9	1051-1097	LNA 151-197G	Ld PDR2/1	PR	H76D	to SELNEC	C
	2051-2097	LNA 251-297G	Dr CRG6LX	PR	H75D	to SELNEC	C
1969	213-214	MND 213-214G	Bd VAL70	Pn	C52F	to SELNEC	
1970	1101-1126	NNB 510-535H	Ld PDR2/1	PR	H75D	new to SELNEC	A
1969/70	1131-1142	NNB 536-547H	Ld PDR2/1	EL	H79F	to SELNEC	B
	1143-1154	NNB 548-559H	Ld PDR2/1	EL	H73D	new to SELNEC	
	2101-2144	NNB 560-603H	Dr CRG6LXB	PR	H75D	new to SELNEC	D

A 1101 onwards had raised driving position. 1117-26 had fully automatic gearboxes
B 1132/6/7/9/40/2 new to SELNEC
C body order placed with Metro Cammell and subcontracted by them to Park Royal
D 2140-2144 had fully automatic gearboxes

1970	1161-1194	ONF 849-882H	Ld PDR2/1	PR	H75D	new to SELNEC in orange livery	B
1970/1	2151-2210	ONF 883-893H PNA 201-249J	Dr CRG6LXB	MC	H77D	new to SELNEC in orange livery	
1971/2	2211-2270	RNA 211-270J	Dr CRG6LXB	PR	H76D	new to SELNEC in orange livery	
	2271-2304	SVR 271-304K	Dr CRG6LXB	Roe	H76D	new to SELNEC in orange livery	A

A body order placed with East Lancs but passed to Park Royal and then Roe due to 1970 fire at East Lancs' factory
B 1193 had a fully automatic gearbox

Vehicles to SELNEC

In service	single-deck	46-99,101-110
	coach	201-214
	Mancunian	1001-1048, 1051-1097, 1131/3/4/5/8/41, 2001-2048, 2051-2097
	Ld double-deck	3200-23/5-64, 3287/94/99, 3323, 3331/32/34/37/39/40/42/45-47/50-52/54/56-60/64, 3411-3792, 3801-3860
	Dr double-deck	4111/18/22-37/39-48/50-74/76-89, 4400-4684, 4701-4760
In driving school		3163/4/97, 3266/71/5/8/8/90, 3324/5, 4101
Withdrawn		3124/38/66/91, 3265/67/69/70/72/77-79/82/89/92/95-97, 3324 4106-08/12-16/19/21

Delivered new to SELNEC

Mancunian	1101-1120 in red with Manchester crests and fleet name
	1121-1126 in red with no crest or fleetname
	1132/6/7/9/40/2-54 in red with Manchester crest and fleetname
	1161-1194 in orange
	2101-2144 in red with Manchester crest and fleetname
	2151-2304 in orange